WISDOM CHRISTOLOGY

Wisdom in Proverbs and the Person of Christ

Dr. Maxwell Shimba

Printed by Shimba Publishing LLC
Printed in the United States of America

TABLE OF CONTENTS

THE CALL OF WISDOM

Wisdom has been treasured across cultures and centuries, revered not just as an abstract concept but as the foundation of a well-lived life. In biblical terms, wisdom is described as the ability to use knowledge rightly, applying it with discernment and understanding at the precise time and place. But what does the Bible reveal about wisdom's nature, its origins, and its value to humanity? Proverbs Chapter 8 offers one of the most profound explorations of wisdom, personifying her as a woman calling out to all who will listen, inviting them to gain insight into God's ways.

The Hebrew word used for wisdom in Proverbs, chokmah (חָכְמָה, Strong's H2451), signifies not only knowledge but the skill of applying it practically. This is wisdom that extends beyond mental acuity, becoming the craft of living rightly. The aim of this study is to bring out the rich layers of meaning in Proverbs 8, expanding upon wisdom's eternal role, practical benefits, and connection to our relationship with God.

Verse-by-Verse Commentary on Proverbs 8

Verse 1: "Does not wisdom call out? Does not understanding raise her voice?"

Here, the call of wisdom is not a whisper but a powerful, public proclamation. The Hebrew word for call here, qara (קָרָא, Strong's H7121), suggests a loud, purposeful invitation. Wisdom does not hide but calls openly, seeking those who will pay attention. We see in this verse that wisdom, embodied as a voice of reason and discernment, is reaching out to humanity, willing to teach and guide anyone willing to listen. Understanding (Hebrew: tebunah, Strong's H8394) is joined with wisdom in the appeal, implying that true wisdom is intertwined with an in-depth comprehension.

Verse 2: "At the highest point along the way, where the paths meet, she takes her stand;"

Wisdom positions herself strategically at a high point—visible to all and calling to those who are at a crossroads in life. The highest point, or the top (Hebrew: rosh, רֹאשׁ, Strong's H7218), signifies a place of prominence.

This location illustrates that wisdom is not hidden in obscure places but is available to anyone willing to seek her guidance, especially at pivotal moments when decisions must be made. Wisdom here is portrayed as accessible and public, waiting for us to come to her when we reach the forks in our paths.

Verse 3: "Beside the gate leading into the city, at the entrance, she cries aloud:"

In ancient cities, the gate was the center of public life, a place for discussions, judgments, and crucial decisions. Wisdom is pictured here at the city's entrance, where people of influence would gather to deliberate on matters of justice and commerce. Her cry is urgent and unmistakable, a call to turn away from folly and embrace understanding. Wisdom's position at the gate reminds us that her influence reaches into public, social, and community life, not limited to personal guidance alone.

Wisdom's Invitation to All

Verse 4: "To you, O people, I call out; I raise my voice to all mankind."

Wisdom's call is universal. This invitation isn't selective or exclusive; it's open to all of humanity, irrespective of background, social status, or prior knowledge. In the

Hebrew, the word adam (אָדָם, Strong's H120) refers to mankind as a whole, emphasizing the inclusivity of wisdom's reach. Wisdom's desire is to impart her knowledge and guidance to everyone who will heed her call, underscoring that no one is beyond the reach of understanding.

Verse 5: "You who are simple, gain prudence; you who are foolish, set your hearts on it."

Wisdom addresses the "simple" (pethiy, פֶּתִי, Strong's H6612), or those who are naive and easily led. She offers them the opportunity to become prudent, (arum, עָרוּם, Strong's H6175), a word that suggests cleverness and shrewdness. Here, wisdom doesn't shame or exclude those who lack understanding; rather, she invites them to grow, to develop discernment. This invitation extends to the foolish, encouraging them to "set their hearts" on wisdom. This phrase implies an intentional turning toward wisdom with a commitment to seek understanding.

The Value of Wisdom Over Wealth

Verse 10: "Choose my instruction instead of silver, knowledge rather than choice gold,"

In a world that often equates wealth with worth, wisdom presents a countercultural truth: her instruction is more valuable than silver, and her knowledge surpasses even the finest gold. The Hebrew word for choose (בָּחַר, bachar, Strong's H977) implies a deliberate act of selection, indicating that wisdom is something we must pursue consciously. In biblical terms, wealth often represented stability and blessing, but here wisdom's value transcends material wealth, as it holds the power to guide us through life with enduring peace and fulfillment.

Verse 11: "For wisdom is more precious than rubies, and nothing you desire can compare with her."

Rubies, like other precious stones, were symbols of rare value and beauty. Yet, wisdom declares herself as more precious than any earthly treasure. The Hebrew word for precious, yaqar (יָקָר, Strong's H3368), speaks to wisdom's intrinsic worth, which surpasses even the deepest desires of the heart. This verse invites us to realign our desires, understanding that nothing we long for compares to the depth, peace, and life that wisdom provides.

Wisdom's Role in Creation

Verse 22: "The Lord brought me forth as the first of his works, before his deeds of old."

Proverbs 8 takes a profound turn here, as wisdom speaks of her origin, proclaiming that the Lord created her as the first of His works. This remarkable statement suggests that wisdom is not an afterthought but was integral to creation itself. The Hebrew phrase for "brought me forth" (qanah, קָנָה, Strong's H7069) can mean "created" or "acquired." In this context, it indicates that wisdom existed before creation, predating time and space, underscoring her eternal nature.

Verse 23: "I was formed long ages ago, at the very beginning, when the world came to be."

This verse reinforces the preexistence of wisdom, showing that she was there even before the creation of the earth. In Hebrew, olam (עוֹלָם, Strong's H5769) often translates to "eternal" or "from ancient times," suggesting wisdom's existence from eternity. Wisdom's presence at creation implies that God's actions in forming the universe were guided by an intricate design. This opens a new understanding for us—recognizing that the very structure of creation is woven with the order and precision of wisdom.

Verse 30-31: "Then I was constantly at his side. I was filled with delight day after day, rejoicing always in his presence, rejoicing in his whole world and delighting in mankind."

Wisdom was not only present at creation but delighted in it. The Hebrew word for "delight" (sachaq, שָׂחַק, Strong's

H7832) means to laugh or rejoice. This implies that wisdom did not view creation as a mere task but as a joyful, collaborative act with God. She rejoiced in both the world and humanity, underscoring the purpose and beauty with which God crafted life. Wisdom's joy is a reminder that God's creation, including humanity, is not just good but precious, full of divine purpose and meaning.

Embracing the Call of Wisdom

The invitation from Proverbs 8 is clear: wisdom is calling, available to all who will listen and seek her diligently. Her eternal nature, her presence in creation, and her priceless worth all point to wisdom as a guide, a friend, and a partner in navigating life. As we heed wisdom's call, let us remember that her value far exceeds anything the world can offer and that her ways lead us closer to the heart of God Himself.

DR. MAXWELL SHIMBA

CHAPTER 01

WISDOM'S ETERNAL PRESENCE

"The Lord brought me forth as the first of his works, before his deeds of old; I was formed long ages ago, at the very beginning, when the world came to be." — Proverbs 8:22-23

In Proverbs 8:22-23, we encounter a profound truth: wisdom existed before the formation of the world, positioned at the very beginning of creation. This passage presents wisdom not as a human-made concept but as an eternal, divine principle. It was established by God and embedded within the fabric of creation itself. The idea that wisdom predates creation offers a transformational view of its importance, aligning it as essential to understanding God's ways and purposes.

To gain insight into this, we will break down the original Hebrew, dive into cross-references, and examine how wisdom's eternal presence influences our perspective on the world and our own lives.

1. The Origin of Wisdom

The phrase "The Lord brought me forth as the first of his works" uses the Hebrew word qanah (קָנָה, Strong's H7069), which can mean "to create," "to possess," or "to acquire." This implies that wisdom was the first of God's creative actions. Here, we understand wisdom as being inherently part of God's nature, not created as something external but brought forth from within God's very being. In other words, wisdom is the essence and expression of God's nature.

Exegesis of qanah

- Qanah is used throughout the Old Testament to imply possession or ownership, such as in Genesis 4:1 when Eve says, "I have gotten (acquired) a man with the help of the Lord."

- In Proverbs 8:22, qanah speaks to the intrinsic relationship wisdom has with God. Rather than a separate entity, wisdom is something that God "possesses" or "acquires" as a natural extension of His nature.

This means that wisdom is not an independent power but one that originates from God. Understanding wisdom as God's possession reshapes our understanding of how we relate to it. Seeking wisdom, therefore, becomes an act of connecting with God's nature.

2. Wisdom as Ancient and Preexistent

The verse continues, "I was formed long ages ago, at the very beginning, when the world came to be." The Hebrew here—olam (עוֹלָם, Strong's H5769)—is often translated as "ages" or "eternity," indicating that wisdom has no beginning or end. Here, wisdom's preexistence is emphasized, showing that it is not bound by time.

Exegesis of olam

- Olam implies something that endures perpetually. This word frequently appears in Psalms to denote God's eternal attributes, such as in Psalm 90:2, "From everlasting (olam) to everlasting you are God."

- By using olam to describe wisdom's origin, Proverbs 8:23 aligns wisdom with the eternal qualities of God Himself.

This preexistence suggests that wisdom is foundational, woven into creation. It predates humanity and was present "when the world came to be." Wisdom, therefore, is not just practical knowledge; it is a divine reality as old as God Himself. This emphasizes that pursuing wisdom is not about acquiring knowledge alone but about connecting with a timeless aspect of God's nature.

3. Wisdom's Role in Creation

Moving forward in Proverbs 8, verses 27-31 describe wisdom's involvement in the act of creation:

- "I was there when he set the heavens in place, when he marked out the horizon on the face of the deep" (Proverbs 8:27).

Wisdom here is pictured as an observer and participant in creation, rejoicing alongside God in His work. This personification of wisdom as being present and active during creation shows that wisdom is deeply embedded in every element of the created world.

Exegesis of chaqaq (to inscribe, Strong's H2710)

- The Hebrew word for "marked out" is chaqaq, which means "to inscribe" or "to carve." This word is often used to describe the action of marking boundaries, as in Job 26:10: "He drew a circular horizon on the face of the waters."

- The use of chaqaq suggests that wisdom is an instrument through which order was brought to the universe, implying that every boundary, from the horizon to the deepest oceans, was crafted through the application of divine wisdom.

Wisdom's role in creation reveals that the universe is not chaotic or random but structured according to divine order. When we seek wisdom, we align ourselves with this underlying order, allowing us to live harmoniously within God's design.

4. The Personification of Wisdom

In Proverbs 8, wisdom is personified as a woman speaking directly to humanity, an image that holds rich theological significance. The personification invites us to see wisdom not as an abstract concept but as something relational and approachable.

Exegesis of chokmah (wisdom, Strong's H2451)

- The Hebrew word for wisdom, chokmah, emphasizes skill and expertise. It is used in Exodus 31:3, where God fills Bezalel with chokmah to design the Tabernacle.

- Chokmah in Proverbs 8 becomes more than skill or knowledge; it is the embodiment of God's principles, inviting us into a personal relationship with His understanding.

By portraying wisdom as calling out and inviting us, Proverbs 8 suggests that wisdom is accessible to all who seek it. The call of wisdom is an invitation to engage with God's creation in a meaningful way, understanding it through His perspective.

5. How Understanding Wisdom's Eternal Presence Shapes Our Lives

If wisdom existed before all things, then it must also govern all things. This insight compels us to seek wisdom as our guiding principle, knowing that it leads us into alignment with God's design for creation. Pursuing wisdom becomes an act of discipleship, an intentional choice to live according to divine principles rather than our own.

Proverbs 8:35-36 warns, "For those who find me find life and receive favor from the Lord. But those who fail to find me harm themselves." Here, we see wisdom's role as essential to our well-being and relationship with God. To live without wisdom is to live out of sync with God's will and order, leading to harm. Thus, wisdom is not only practical but necessary for a life in alignment with God's purpose.

Reflection and Application

In reflecting on wisdom as eternal and integral to creation, we are called to reassess how we value and pursue it:

1. Pursue Wisdom as a Reflection of God's Nature

Since wisdom originates from God, seeking it is akin to seeking God Himself. When we pursue wisdom, we are not merely gathering knowledge but growing closer to God's heart and understanding.

2. Align with the Order of Creation

Recognizing wisdom's role in creation encourages us to live in harmony with God's design. When we apply wisdom, we engage in a form of worship, respecting and honoring the order God established.

3. Wisdom as a Guide in Decision-Making

Knowing that wisdom was present at the formation of all things means it is relevant to every decision we face. Just as God used wisdom to set the heavens in place, we too can use wisdom as a guide in structuring our lives.

4. Seek Wisdom in Humility and Reverence

Proverbs 9:10 tells us, "The fear of the Lord is the beginning of wisdom." To truly embrace wisdom, we must approach God with reverence, recognizing His authority over our lives and creation.

Wisdom's eternal presence teaches us that it is foundational, purposeful, and central to God's design. In seeking wisdom, we connect with a divine principle that transcends time, inviting us to participate in God's order and purpose for creation. Embracing wisdom is not merely an intellectual endeavor but a spiritual journey, aligning us with God's will and allowing us to live lives that reflect His eternal truth.

Wisdom's Eternal Presence — A Theological Perspective

In exploring wisdom's eternal presence, Proverbs 8 offers a powerful theological vision of wisdom as not merely a human trait or concept, but as an intrinsic, divine attribute that transcends time and creation. From a theological perspective, the depiction of wisdom in Proverbs 8 gives insight into God's nature and purpose, revealing wisdom as a foundational element woven into the fabric of existence. This chapter will delve into theological interpretations of wisdom's origin, character, and role in creation, with an emphasis on how these aspects impact our understanding of God and the spiritual pursuit of wisdom.

1. Wisdom as Divine Essence: Wisdom "Brought Forth"

In Proverbs 8:22-23, we read, "The Lord brought me forth as the first of his works, before his deeds of old." The Hebrew term here for "brought forth," qanah (קָנָה, Strong's H7069), has significant theological implications. Qanah can mean "to acquire," "to possess," or even "to create," giving this phrase a dual meaning. It suggests that wisdom is both an extension of God's own nature and the first manifestation of His creative will. In this context, wisdom is not just a concept but part of the divine essence, brought into being as the first act of creation, closely aligned with God's own identity.

Theological Implication:

Understanding wisdom as God's possession highlights the divine generosity in offering it to humanity. If wisdom is part of God's essence, then pursuing wisdom is a journey toward knowing God more intimately. God's invitation to seek wisdom is therefore an invitation to connect with His own nature.

2. Wisdom's Eternity and Immutability

Wisdom's presence "long ages ago, at the very beginning" (Proverbs 8:23) suggests a quality of eternality that mirrors God's own timelessness. The term olam (עוֹלָם, Strong's H5769), meaning "forever" or "eternity," affirms that wisdom transcends temporal constraints and is therefore unchanging. Wisdom existed before the foundations of the earth, making it part of the eternal order of things. Theologically, this positions wisdom as an immutable aspect of God that remains steadfast regardless of human circumstances or worldly change.

Theological Implication:

The eternal nature of wisdom suggests that God's truth is unchanging. In a world marked by constant flux and shifting morals, wisdom offers an anchor. Seeking wisdom aligns us with an aspect of God that is eternal, giving us stability and perspective rooted in divine constancy.

3. Wisdom in Creation: The Role of Divine Order

As Proverbs 8:27-29 states, "I was there when he set the heavens in place… when he marked out the foundations of the earth." Wisdom's role in creation reveals God's orderly and purposeful design. The Hebrew words used in these verses emphasize setting boundaries and establishing foundations, depicting wisdom as integral to the stability and order of the universe.

Theologically, this suggests that creation itself is an expression of God's wisdom. The boundaries of creation reflect divine structure and intention, underscoring a world that is not chaotic or arbitrary but infused with meaning. Wisdom, as an agent in this process, illustrates God's desire for an orderly, harmonious creation, where everything has its place.

Theological Implication:

Since wisdom structured the universe, seeking wisdom is also a call to seek order and harmony within ourselves and our communities. Living by wisdom is a way of living in sync with the divine order, fulfilling our roles as God's creation in harmony with His design.

4. Wisdom Personified: An Invitation to Relationship

The personification of wisdom in Proverbs 8 is striking; wisdom speaks and calls out, inviting humanity into a relationship. This personification serves not just as poetic imagery but as theological symbolism, representing wisdom as relational. Wisdom is presented as approachable and accessible, inviting us to receive her counsel.

Theologically, this personification foreshadows Christ as the ultimate embodiment of divine wisdom. In Christian thought, Jesus is often seen as the "Word" (Logos) through whom all things were made (John 1:1-3) and the personification of wisdom (1 Corinthians 1:24). Just as wisdom was present at creation, so was the Word, showing a continuity between the wisdom of Proverbs and the incarnation of Christ.

Theological Implication:

Wisdom's personification invites us to view it not merely as a concept but as a means of relating to God. It is not distant or inaccessible; rather, it beckons us to engage. This relational aspect underscores the personal nature of

God, who desires connection with humanity and offers wisdom as a way to know and love Him more deeply.

5. Wisdom's Call to Participation in Divine Life

If wisdom is part of God's essence and purpose, then humanity's pursuit of wisdom is a call to participate in the divine life. Proverbs 8 presents wisdom as both the pathway to understanding God's nature and the means by which we can reflect His image. By seeking wisdom, we align ourselves with God's vision and bring our own lives into harmony with His purposes.

In Christian theology, this pursuit finds fulfillment in the indwelling of the Holy Spirit, who imparts wisdom and understanding to believers (Ephesians 1:17). Wisdom's eternal presence therefore not only draws us to God but also empowers us to live in a way that mirrors His truth, justice, and love.

Theological Implication:

Our pursuit of wisdom is more than an intellectual endeavor; it is a spiritual discipline that draws us into communion with God. By living wisely, we not only reflect God's nature but actively participate in His divine work in the world, bringing light, order, and peace.

Reflection and Application

This theological view of wisdom as eternal, relational, and part of God's nature invites us to reconsider how we approach wisdom in our own lives:

1. Wisdom as a Pathway to Know God

Recognizing wisdom as God's essence elevates it from mere knowledge to a divine encounter. When we seek wisdom, we seek God Himself. This makes the pursuit of wisdom a sacred act, where each step toward wisdom is a step closer to understanding God's character.

2. Living in Harmony with Divine Order

Since wisdom was foundational in creation, living wisely means living in harmony with God's order. Pursuing wisdom encourages us to value integrity, balance, and purpose in every aspect of life.

3. Viewing Wisdom as Relationship, Not Just Knowledge

The personification of wisdom as one who calls to us suggests that wisdom is meant to be relational. It invites us to an ongoing dialogue with God, where wisdom becomes a guide and companion, reflecting the deeply personal nature of God's engagement with us.

4. Participating in God's Creative Work

Seeking wisdom aligns us with God's work in creation and restoration. As we embody wisdom, we become agents of God's order, justice, and love in a world that often lacks these qualities. Wisdom enables us to join in God's mission to redeem and renew all things.

In conclusion, Proverbs 8 offers a rich theological perspective on wisdom as eternal and integral to God's nature. Wisdom is not a distant ideal but a divine attribute that permeates creation and invites us into relationship. As we grow in wisdom, we grow in understanding God's ways, participating in His life, and bringing His truth and harmony into the world around us. Through wisdom, we experience not only the mind of God but the heart of God—a heart that calls us to seek, to know, and to live in His love.

Wisdom as an Eternal Attribute of God

Is wisdom part of God's eternal attributes? The Scriptures, particularly the Old Testament, portray wisdom as intrinsic to God's very nature—eternal, foundational, and manifested through creation, law, and divine order. Proverbs 8 presents wisdom as "Lady Wisdom," a personification revealing God's will and ways in the world He made. By examining this passage and related texts, we gain insight into wisdom not only as a divine characteristic but as an enduring, integral attribute of God's nature.

1. Wisdom as God's Eternal Attribute in Creation

Proverbs 8 provides one of the clearest portrayals of wisdom as an eternal aspect of God. In Proverbs 8:22-23, wisdom declares, "The Lord possessed me at the beginning of his work, the first of his acts of old. Ages ago I was set up, at the first, before the beginning of the earth." Here, the Hebrew word qanah (קָנָה, Strong's H7069), translated as "possessed" or "acquired," suggests that wisdom has been a part of God's being since the beginning. This expression aligns with the concept of wisdom as an eternal attribute— something that pre-exists creation and is inseparable from God's identity.

Expository Insight: The Role of Wisdom in Creation

The following verses in Proverbs 8:27-30 describe wisdom's involvement in God's creative acts: "When He established the heavens, I was there... when He marked out the foundations of the earth, then I was beside Him, like a master workman." Here, the term master workman (amon, אָמוֹן, Strong's H525), suggests a skilled artisan or architect. Wisdom, portrayed as God's co-laborer in creation, affirms the order, precision, and intentionality that God embedded in the universe.

Theological Implication:

Wisdom is not simply a tool or quality God uses; it is central to His nature and His creative process. Viewing wisdom as part of God's essence suggests that creation itself reflects divine wisdom, purpose, and order. Just as creation manifests God's power, it also reveals His wisdom, providing humanity with a glimpse into God's character.

2. Wisdom Revealed in Divine Law and Order

Wisdom also appears in God's law, where it functions as a guide for righteous living. In Deuteronomy 4:6, Moses urges Israel to "keep and do [God's statutes and judgments], for that will be your wisdom and understanding in the sight of the nations." The word for "wisdom" here is chokmah (חָכְמָה, Strong's H2451), which implies both skill and discernment. God's laws were given not only as rules but as expressions of divine wisdom that would set His people apart and reveal His character to the world.

Expository Insight: Wisdom in the Law

The link between wisdom and the law shows that God's commandments are not arbitrary but reflect His order and design. In keeping God's statutes, Israel could live in alignment with the wisdom present in creation, harmonizing with the divine purpose established from the beginning. Psalm 19:7 echoes this truth, stating, "The law of the Lord is perfect, reviving the soul; the testimony of the Lord is sure, making wise the simple." Here, the law is a conduit of wisdom, offering instruction that brings life, understanding, and spiritual insight.

Theological Implication:

When we see God's wisdom in the law, we understand that obedience is not about restriction but about aligning with God's wise and purposeful design. Following God's commandments leads us to live within His will, allowing us to partake in the order and harmony God intended for His creation.

3. Lady Wisdom: Personification and Invitation

In Proverbs 8, wisdom is personified as a woman—Lady Wisdom—who calls out to humanity. This personification serves a theological purpose, as it portrays wisdom as accessible, relational, and inviting. Proverbs 8:1-4 opens with, "Does not wisdom call out? Does not understanding raise her voice?... To you, O people, I call out; I raise my voice to all mankind." The depiction of wisdom as a figure reaching out to humanity emphasizes that wisdom is meant to be sought and embraced.

Expository Insight: Wisdom as a Divine Call

The Hebrew word for "call" here is qara (קָרָא, Strong's H7121), which implies an invitation or summoning. Lady Wisdom does not remain distant; she actively engages, urging people to pursue her and gain insight. This portrayal reinforces the idea that God desires a relationship with humanity, inviting them to share in His wisdom and thus grow closer to His nature.

Theological Implication:

The personification of wisdom as Lady Wisdom suggests that wisdom is not a detached quality of God but a means by which He draws people into understanding and fellowship. Through wisdom, God provides guidance, clarity, and direction, calling humanity to a life that mirrors His truth and goodness.

4. Wisdom's Eternality and Relationship with God's Other Attributes

Wisdom's eternal presence in God's nature connects it with His other attributes, such as love, justice, and power. In Job 38, God responds to Job's questions about suffering by emphasizing His wisdom in creation: "Who marked off its dimensions? Surely you know! Who stretched a measuring line across it?" (Job 38:5). Here, God's wisdom is inseparable from His power and sovereignty, underscoring that His governance of the universe is wise and purposeful.

Expository Insight: The Harmony of Divine Attributes

The Hebrew term tebunah (תְּבוּנָה, Strong's H8394), translated as "understanding," is often associated with wisdom in the Old Testament and emphasizes discernment and insight. In the context of God's attributes, tebunah reflects the harmonious balance of wisdom with justice and love, suggesting that God's actions are motivated by both knowledge and compassion.

Theological Implication:

God's wisdom is always in alignment with His love and justice, creating a perfect balance that ensures His actions are both good and right. Wisdom, then, is an attribute that brings coherence to God's character and actions, showing that His decisions are not only powerful but just and compassionate.

5. The Pursuit of Divine Wisdom as Participation in God's Nature

If wisdom is an eternal attribute of God, then the pursuit of wisdom is a call to participate in the divine life. Proverbs 9:10 states, "The fear of the Lord is the beginning of wisdom, and knowledge of the Holy One is understanding." The phrase "fear of the Lord" (yirah, יִרְאָה, Strong's H3374) denotes reverence and respect, pointing to a relationship with God that acknowledges His greatness and seeks alignment with His will.

Expository Insight: The Call to Seek Wisdom

The fear of the Lord as the foundation of wisdom suggests that true wisdom begins with humility and recognition of our dependence on God. By revering God, we open ourselves to His guidance and embrace the wisdom that is part of His eternal nature.

Theological Implication:

In seeking wisdom, we participate in God's nature, gaining insight, understanding, and moral clarity. The pursuit of wisdom becomes an act of worship, aligning our lives with the divine order and reflecting God's attributes in our actions. Wisdom, then, is not merely an intellectual pursuit; it is a path to spiritual transformation and communion with God.

Reflection and Application

The understanding of wisdom as part of God's eternal attributes has profound implications for our lives:

1. Viewing Wisdom as Sacred

If wisdom is part of God's essence, seeking wisdom becomes an act of reverence. Wisdom is more than practical insight; it is a spiritual pursuit that draws us closer to the divine.

2. Aligning with Divine Order

Since wisdom structured creation, living wisely is living in harmony with God's design. Obedience to God's wisdom leads to a life of order, purpose, and peace.

3. Responding to God's Invitation

Lady Wisdom's call is an invitation to relationship. Pursuing wisdom means responding to God's call and drawing nearer to His truth.

4. Reflecting God's Character

As wisdom encompasses justice, love, and power, our pursuit of wisdom helps us embody these qualities, reflecting God's character in our actions.

In conclusion, wisdom is indeed an eternal attribute of God, present before creation and manifesting throughout Scripture as part of His divine nature. Proverbs 8 and other passages reveal that wisdom is integral to God's character, not just a tool for guidance but a part of His very essence. As we seek wisdom, we enter into a deeper relationship with God, aligning our lives with His eternal truth and participating in His divine purpose.

CHAPTER 02

THE VALUE OF WISDOM

"Choose my instruction instead of silver, knowledge rather than choice gold, for wisdom is more precious than rubies, and nothing you desire can compare with her."

— Proverbs 8:10-11

In today's society, wealth is often equated with success and security. Gold, silver, and precious stones—symbols of earthly wealth—hold significant allure, but Proverbs 8 shifts our focus. The call of Lady Wisdom in verses 10-11 reveals that wisdom surpasses even the most prized possessions. This chapter examines the profound value of wisdom in contrast with material wealth, highlighting how wisdom provides eternal rewards beyond what money can buy.

1. Wisdom versus Material Wealth: An Eternal Perspective

Proverbs 8:10 encourages us to "choose my instruction instead of silver, knowledge rather than choice gold." The Hebrew word for "instruction" (musar, מוּסָר, Strong's H4148) refers to correction, discipline, or moral teaching. This word implies that wisdom guides us not only in gaining knowledge but also in developing character, shaping us to live rightly. While silver and gold may bring temporary satisfaction, wisdom leads to lasting transformation and a life aligned with God's will.

Expository Insight: Choosing Wisdom Over Wealth

In this passage, "knowledge" is paired with "choice gold" to emphasize the comparison between intellectual and material wealth. The Hebrew term for "knowledge" (da'ath, דַעַת, Strong's H1847) often refers to a deeper, experiential understanding rather than mere intellectual awareness. True knowledge, grounded in wisdom, enriches the soul, while material wealth serves only temporary purposes.

Theological Implication:

God calls us to seek wisdom not for selfish gain but to live in alignment with His truth. Earthly treasures may seem valuable, but wisdom offers something that lasts beyond life's fleeting pursuits. By choosing wisdom, we prioritize eternal over temporal riches.

2. Wisdom's Superiority to Worldly Riches

Proverbs 8:11 states, "for wisdom is more precious than rubies, and nothing you desire can compare with her." Here, wisdom is likened to rubies, a rare and valuable gem in ancient times. The Hebrew term for "rubies" (peninim, פְּנִינִים, Strong's H6443) can also mean "precious stones." By placing wisdom above even the finest treasures, the text underscores its incomparable worth.

Expository Insight: True Wealth in Wisdom

This verse not only speaks to wisdom's intrinsic value but also contrasts it with desires that often drive human ambition. The phrase "nothing you desire" (chepes, חֵפֶץ, Strong's H2656) represents any form of earthly desire or pleasure. No matter how enticing earthly possessions may appear, they pale in comparison to the depth, peace, and fulfillment that come with wisdom.

Theological Implication:

Worldly riches are ultimately transient, but wisdom carries a value that endures. Godly wisdom enriches our lives in ways material wealth cannot, bringing peace, direction, and spiritual insight. As we grow in wisdom, our desires align with God's, leading us toward a life of purpose and lasting fulfillment.

3. The Riches of Wisdom in God's Sight

Scripture consistently elevates the worth of wisdom above material wealth. In Job 28:18, we read, "Coral and jasper are not worthy of mention; the price of wisdom is beyond rubies." Job, having suffered the loss of all earthly goods, understands that wisdom holds an eternal value transcending earthly treasures.

In the New Testament, this theme is reiterated by James 3:17, which says, "But the wisdom from above is first pure, then peaceable, gentle, open to reason, full of mercy and good fruits, impartial and sincere." The attributes of divine wisdom here show that it produces a wealth of character that far exceeds material gain.

Expository Insight: Wisdom as a Reflection of God's Character

The qualities of wisdom—purity, peace, mercy, and sincerity—reflect God's own character. When we value wisdom, we are valuing the very nature of God, aligning ourselves with His purposes rather than the fleeting rewards of material success.

Theological Implication:

Wisdom is an eternal treasure because it brings us closer to God. Earthly riches can distract us from spiritual growth, but wisdom opens our hearts to God's ways, offering us riches that neither rust nor fade. The pursuit of wisdom is thus a pursuit of God Himself, seeking a life that mirrors His holiness and grace.

4. A Warning Against Trusting in Material Wealth

While wisdom is shown to be invaluable, the Bible also warns against the dangers of placing trust in material wealth. In Proverbs 11:4, it says, "Riches do not profit in the day of wrath, but righteousness delivers from death." Here, "riches" (hon, הוֹן, Strong's H1952) is contrasted with "righteousness" (tsedaqah, צְדָקָה, Strong's H6666), which is closely related to living wisely. Earthly wealth holds no power in the face of ultimate judgment, but wisdom that leads to righteous living offers deliverance.

Expository Insight: The Temporary Nature of Wealth

Earthly riches are often pursued as a form of security, but this verse reveals the illusion of such security. Material wealth may provide comfort or prestige, but it cannot save a soul or grant peace with God. Wisdom, on the other hand, guides us toward righteousness and the eternal security found in a relationship with God.

Theological Implication:

The pursuit of wealth without wisdom can lead to emptiness, while a life guided by wisdom leads to true security and peace. By seeking wisdom, we invest in what truly matters and prepare for eternity rather than merely seeking temporal comfort.

5. True Prosperity: The Fruit of Wisdom

Proverbs 8:18-19 states, "With me are riches and honor, enduring wealth and prosperity. My fruit is better than fine gold; what I yield surpasses choice silver." Here, wisdom speaks of its "fruit" (peri, פְּרִי, Strong's H6529), a metaphor for the outcomes or blessings that result from living wisely. This fruit surpasses fine gold or choice silver, indicating that the benefits of wisdom are not only material but also spiritual and relational.

Expository Insight: The Prosperity of Wisdom

The "riches and honor" associated with wisdom in these verses signify a kind of wealth that goes beyond material gain. True prosperity—defined by contentment, honor, and righteous living—is a natural result of embracing wisdom. This prosperity is enduring, not subject to market fluctuations or earthly decay, because it is rooted in God's eternal truth.

Theological Implication:

God blesses those who seek His wisdom with a form of wealth that cannot be diminished or lost. This doesn't imply a prosperity gospel but speaks to the inner riches of peace, integrity, and spiritual fulfillment that wisdom brings. In this way, wisdom offers us a taste of God's eternal riches, leading us to true prosperity in His presence.

6. Application: Pursuing Wisdom in a Wealth-Obsessed World

In Matthew 6:19-20, Jesus instructs, "Do not store up for yourselves treasures on earth, where moths and vermin destroy, and where thieves break in and steal. But store up for yourselves treasures in heaven, where moths and vermin do not destroy, and where thieves do not break in and steal." The pursuit of wisdom, rather than material wealth, aligns with storing up "heavenly treasures"—eternal values and virtues that reflect God's kingdom.

Expository Insight: The Choice Before Us

The Hebrew concept of wisdom involves both knowledge and action. To truly value wisdom, we must let it shape our choices, directing us away from worldly ambitions and toward a life of service, humility, and integrity.

Theological Implication:

Pursuing wisdom means reorienting our lives around God's values rather than society's standards. True wealth lies not in what we accumulate but in who we become. By choosing wisdom, we prioritize God's kingdom, ultimately finding that wisdom provides everything we need and more.

The value of wisdom surpasses even the most treasured earthly riches. Proverbs 8 teaches us that wisdom is more precious than gold, silver, and rubies, offering a form of wealth that endures beyond the grave. While material wealth may bring temporary satisfaction, wisdom provides eternal rewards, aligning us with God's will, enriching our character, and leading to a life of true prosperity. As we choose wisdom, we choose a life that reflects God's nature, investing in treasures that cannot be lost. Wisdom's riches are freely offered, waiting for those who seek her to inherit a wealth beyond measure.

Where Faith and Wisdom Meet

The Bible places a strong emphasis on both faith and wisdom as essential virtues for those who seek to follow God. Wisdom is woven throughout the Old Testament, especially in the books of Proverbs, Ecclesiastes, and Job, while faith takes center stage in the New Testament. Wisdom is referenced approximately 218 times, and faith about 270 times—each highlighting unique but complementary aspects of a life dedicated to God. This chapter explores the dynamic interplay between faith and wisdom, emphasizing that both are crucial for a balanced and fulfilling walk with Christ.

1. The Complementary Roles of Faith and Wisdom

While faith and wisdom may appear distinct, they are not opposing forces but rather partners in the life of a believer. Faith is often defined as "the assurance of things hoped for, the conviction of things not seen" (Hebrews 11:1), while wisdom, according to Proverbs 4:7, is "the principal thing; therefore get wisdom." Faith requires trust in the unseen and a willingness to step beyond human understanding, while wisdom brings discernment, clarity, and alignment with God's will.

Expository Insight:

The Hebrew word for faith (emunah, אֱמוּנָה, Strong's H530) implies steadfastness, firmness, and fidelity. It is more than belief; it is a deep-rooted trust in God's character. On the other hand, the Hebrew word for wisdom (chokmah, חָכְמָה, Strong's H2451) refers to skill, insight, or applied knowledge. Both attributes reflect aspects of God's character, showing that a life rooted in Christ should incorporate both a trusting faith and a discerning wisdom.

Theological Implication:

Just as faith without works is dead (James 2:17), faith without wisdom can lead to missteps and confusion. Wisdom guides faith, showing us how to apply our trust in God to the daily decisions and challenges we face. Thus, faith and wisdom are not merely abstract virtues; they are practical tools that equip us to live righteously in a complex world.

2. Faith Leads Us to Seek Wisdom

The Bible repeatedly links a reverent faith in God with the pursuit of wisdom. Proverbs 9:10 states, "The fear of the

Lord is the beginning of wisdom, and knowledge of the Holy One is understanding." This "fear of the Lord" (yirah, יִרְאָה, Strong's H3374) is an awe-filled reverence, a recognition of God's sovereignty, which leads us to seek His wisdom. Faith, therefore, is the starting point of wisdom because it acknowledges God as the ultimate source of all understanding and guidance.

Expository Insight: Faith Inspires the Pursuit of Wisdom

Faith is not merely a belief in God's existence but an active dependence on His character and promises. When we have faith in God, we naturally desire to know His ways, which leads us to wisdom. As Proverbs 2:6 says, "For the Lord gives wisdom; from his mouth come knowledge and understanding." Faith drives us to seek this divine wisdom as we look to God for guidance.

Theological Implication:

Faith without wisdom may lead to zeal without knowledge, but wisdom grounded in faith becomes an instrument of God's grace. Faith calls us to trust God; wisdom shows us how to trust in practical and informed ways.

This partnership enables us to make decisions that honor God and reflect His love in our actions.

3. Wisdom as the Expression of Faith in Action

Faith without wisdom can easily drift into presumption, while wisdom without faith can become worldly and self-reliant. James 1:5-6 reminds believers, "If any of you lacks wisdom, let him ask of God...but let him ask in faith, with no doubting." Here, James connects faith with the act of seeking wisdom, showing that wisdom should be sought with the confidence that God will provide it.

Expository Insight: Asking in Faith for Wisdom

In this passage, the Greek word for "ask" (aiteo, αἰτέω, Strong's G154) is a term that implies persistence and expectancy. To ask for wisdom in faith is to believe not only in God's ability to provide but also in His willingness to guide us. This faith-filled request aligns our heart with God's, ensuring that the wisdom we receive will be used to honor Him.

Theological Implication:

Seeking wisdom in faith acknowledges that human knowledge alone is insufficient. True wisdom is a divine gift, meant to direct us according to God's purposes. When we ask for wisdom with unwavering faith, we are empowered to act on that wisdom with courage and trust, embodying our faith in every choice and action.

4. The Dangers of Wisdom Without Faith

Scripture warns of the dangers of wisdom apart from faith. James 3:15 describes a "wisdom" that is "earthly, unspiritual, and demonic," a counterfeit wisdom rooted in self-interest rather than divine truth. This earthly wisdom leads to envy and discord, as it lacks the grounding of faith in God's character.

Expository Insight: Earthly Versus Heavenly Wisdom

James contrasts "earthly wisdom" with the "wisdom that comes from above" (James 3:17). This "heavenly" wisdom is "pure, peaceable, gentle, open to reason, full of mercy and good fruits, impartial and sincere." Heavenly wisdom reflects the heart of God and leads to peace and righteousness, whereas earthly wisdom is tainted by pride and ambition.

Theological Implication:

Wisdom devoid of faith is not true wisdom but a distortion of it. Faith provides the humility needed to seek wisdom that serves God rather than self. Without faith, wisdom can become a source of pride, but with faith, it becomes a path to godliness.

5. How Faith and Wisdom Work Together in Decision-Making

Faith and wisdom together guide our decisions, providing a balance between trust in God's sovereignty and responsible stewardship of our lives. Proverbs 3:5-6 encourages us to "Trust in the Lord with all your heart and lean not on your own understanding; in all your ways submit to him, and he will make your paths straight." This passage shows that while faith in God is paramount, wisdom directs us to align our actions with that trust.

Expository Insight: Balancing Faith and Understanding

To "lean not on your own understanding" is not a call to abandon wisdom but to recognize its limits apart from God. Godly wisdom works alongside faith, ensuring that our understanding does not become self-reliant but remains rooted in reverence for God. When faith and wisdom work in harmony, we are empowered to make wise choices that honor God's plan.

Theological Implication:

Decisions rooted in both faith and wisdom demonstrate a mature understanding of God's guidance. Faith leads us to trust God's providence, while wisdom allows us to apply that trust in practical ways. This balanced approach ensures that our decisions are not reckless but grounded in a respect for God's ways.

6. Examples of Faith and Wisdom in Scripture

he Bible is rich with examples of faith and wisdom working in harmony. One of the most notable is King Solomon, who, when offered anything by God, chose wisdom (1 Kings 3:9). His faith in God's ability to guide him led to his request for wisdom, and as a result, he was blessed with both wisdom and prosperity. Solomon's example demonstrates that when faith seeks wisdom, blessings follow.

Another example is found in Hebrews 11, where the "hall of faith" includes individuals like Noah, who, by faith, acted wisely in preparing an ark (Hebrews 11:7). His faith led him to heed God's warning, and his wisdom in action preserved his family. Faith and wisdom worked together, leading to a life-saving outcome.

Theological Implication:

These examples show that faith alone is not enough; it must inspire us to act wisely. Likewise, wisdom alone is insufficient without faith to guide its application. Together, faith and wisdom bring about God's purposes in our lives, empowering us to live in a way that honors Him.

The Unity of Faith and Wisdom in Following Christ

Faith and wisdom are not merely virtues but essentials for a life devoted to God. Faith calls us to trust in God's character, while wisdom enables us to live in a way that reflects that trust. Proverbs 8:10-11 reminds us that "wisdom is more precious than rubies, and nothing you desire can compare with her." When we pursue wisdom in faith, we find a treasure that not only enriches our lives but also brings us closer to the heart of God.

In a world filled with uncertainty, the partnership of faith and wisdom equips us to navigate challenges, make decisions that honor God, and lead lives of purpose and peace. Let us, therefore, seek wisdom earnestly, grounding our pursuit in a steadfast faith that trusts God to lead us, not only to understanding but to a life that glorifies Him in every way.

CHAPTER 03

WISDOM'S CALL TO EVERYONE

In Proverbs 8:1-3, Wisdom is portrayed as a voice calling out to all who are willing to listen. She stands at the crossroads, in the marketplace, and at the city gates, inviting everyone to receive her guidance. Unlike knowledge that might be reserved for the educated or privileged, wisdom is universal and accessible to all. This chapter will explore how wisdom reaches out to people from all walks of life and the practical implications of responding to her call.

1. The Universality of Wisdom's Call

Verse Reference:

"Does not wisdom call out? Does not understanding raise her voice?" — Proverbs 8:1

In this opening verse, wisdom is depicted as raising her voice, calling out for anyone to heed her message. The question is rhetorical, suggesting that wisdom is active and persistent in seeking the attention of all. Here, wisdom is not exclusive but inclusive, accessible to anyone willing to listen.

Expository Insight:

The Hebrew word for "wisdom" (chokmah, חׇכְמָה, Strong's H2451) conveys the idea of skill and insight, not just intellectual knowledge. The term implies practical knowledge applied rightly. The Hebrew for "understanding" (tebunah, תְּבוּנָה, Strong's H8394) refers to discernment or perception. Together, they emphasize a wisdom that is not theoretical but practical, usable by anyone at any time.

Theological Implication:

The call of wisdom is inclusive. While some may think wisdom is reserved for the educated or privileged, Proverbs 8 shows us that wisdom's call is universal. It is as accessible to the farmer as it is to the scholar. This accessibility underscores God's generosity, inviting all of His creation to partake in His wisdom.

2. The Public Call of Wisdom

Verse Reference:

"At the highest point along the way, where the paths meet, she takes her stand; beside the gate leading into the city, at the entrance, she cries aloud." — Proverbs 8:2-3

Wisdom is depicted here in public places: at the "highest point" (a visible, prominent location), "where the paths meet" (symbolizing crossroads or places of decision), and "at the gate" (the city's entry point where community decisions were made). Wisdom is not hidden in a secluded place but stands openly in the places where people make important choices.

Expository Insight:

The Hebrew for "highest point" (rosh, רֹאשׁ, Strong's H7218) can also mean head or chief, indicating a prominent location. The "paths" (netiyb, נְתִיבָה, Strong's H5410) signify roads or ways, suggesting the many options or decisions people face. The "gate" (sha'ar, שַׁעַר, Strong's H8179) was a place of judgment and commerce, where people gathered for business and legal matters.

Theological Implication:

The visibility of wisdom's call symbolizes God's desire for everyone to seek and know Him. By standing at the gate and at the crossroads, wisdom is strategically positioned where people make decisions, emphasizing that God provides guidance precisely where we need it most. This reminds us that we are never alone in our decision-making; God's wisdom is available to guide us.

3. The Invitation to All Who Will Listen

Wisdom's call is impartial, reaching out to everyone who is willing to hear. Unlike human teachers who might discriminate based on ability or status, wisdom speaks to all, offering her guidance freely. This inclusiveness challenges us to consider whether we are open to receiving wisdom or if we let pride, ignorance, or distractions keep us from hearing her.

Verse Reference:

"To you, O people, I call out; I raise my voice to all mankind." — Proverbs 8:4

Expository Insight:

The Hebrew word for "people" (ben, בֵּן, Strong's H1121) here is often used to refer to all people as children or descendants, emphasizing that wisdom's call is directed to everyone, not just a select few. The use of "mankind" (adam, אָדָם, Strong's H120) implies a universal reach, extending wisdom's invitation to every human being.

Theological Implication:

Wisdom's universal call mirrors God's desire that all people come to know Him (1 Timothy 2:4). This passage shows us that God's wisdom is not confined to one group, nation, or type of person. It is available to all who are open to it. In a world that often divides people, wisdom's call to everyone reflects the unity and equality inherent in God's love.

4. Wisdom at the Crossroads: The Decision Point

Life presents us with many crossroads, moments when we must choose one path over another. Proverbs 8 places wisdom at these decision points, indicating that God's guidance is available to help us navigate choices. The crossroads symbolize critical points in our lives where decisions can lead us closer to or further from God's purpose.

Verse Reference:

"At the crossroads, she takes her stand." — Proverbs 8:2

Expository Insight:

The term "crossroads" (pethach, פֶּתַח, Strong's H6607) implies an opening, a place where paths diverge. Wisdom stands here, inviting us to make choices that align with God's will. The crossroads can represent not only literal life decisions but also spiritual and moral choices.

Theological Implication:

Crossroads are opportunities for growth and refinement. Wisdom calls us at these points, guiding us toward decisions that honor God and benefit us. When we face choices that seem confusing or daunting, we can trust that wisdom is there, offering insight and direction.

5. Receiving Wisdom's Call: Opening Our Hearts and Minds

Receiving wisdom requires openness and humility. Often, people resist wisdom's call, preferring their own ways or fearing change. Yet, Proverbs urges us to listen attentively and to let wisdom guide us, for her ways lead to life and understanding.

Verse Reference:

"Listen, for I have trustworthy things to say; I open my lips to speak what is right." — Proverbs 8:6

Expository Insight:

The word "listen" (shama, שָׁמַע, Strong's H8085) is more than just hearing; it implies paying attention, obeying, and taking to heart. To listen to wisdom is to be receptive and willing to act on what we hear. The call to listen is a call to relationship, to align ourselves with God's ways.

Theological Implication:

The act of listening is a spiritual discipline. Wisdom calls us to be attentive and obedient, cultivating a heart that is open to correction and guidance. As Jesus said in the New Testament, "Whoever has ears, let them hear" (Matthew 11:15). This readiness to hear and respond is crucial to receiving God's wisdom.

6. Making Wisdom Personal: Taking Action on Her Call

Wisdom's call is not only an invitation to hear but also a challenge to act. Receiving wisdom involves not just intellectual understanding but practical application in our lives. God's wisdom is meant to shape our character, influence our decisions, and guide our relationships.

Verse Reference:

"Take my instruction instead of silver, and knowledge rather than choice gold." — Proverbs 8:10

Expository Insight:

The word "instruction" (musar, מוּסָר, Strong's H4148) implies discipline and correction. It suggests that wisdom requires us to be teachable, willing to accept guidance even if it challenges us. Choosing wisdom over silver and gold indicates valuing God's guidance more than worldly wealth.

Theological Implication:

Choosing wisdom means prioritizing God's values over material gains. This is not always easy, but it is the path to true life and fulfillment. Just as Solomon asked for wisdom rather than riches (1 Kings 3:9-13), we are called to seek God's understanding above all else. Responding to wisdom's call transforms our lives, enabling us to live in alignment with God's purposes.

Responding to Wisdom's Call

Wisdom's call is clear and accessible to all. She stands at the crossroads of life, calling out to everyone who will listen and guiding us in the paths of righteousness. Wisdom's universal call reflects God's love for all people, inviting us to make choices that align with His will. As we open our hearts to receive wisdom, we embark on a journey that leads to true understanding, peace, and joy.

The call of wisdom is not passive; it is active and persistent. By seeking wisdom daily, we embrace God's guidance and are empowered to live lives that reflect His character.

Examples of Solomonic Wisdom

The wisdom of King Solomon is legendary, not only in the Bible but also in various traditions around the world. Solomon's wisdom was a divine gift, a unique insight into human nature, justice, and the complexities of life. His wisdom was not just theoretical knowledge but a practical, discerning wisdom applied to real-life situations. This chapter will explore several examples of Solomon's wisdom and how they demonstrate discernment, justice, and compassion, often referred to as "Solomonic wisdom."

1. Solomon's Gift of Wisdom

The foundation of Solomon's wisdom was his unique relationship with God. In 1 Kings 3, Solomon famously asked God for a discerning heart to govern God's people. Instead of asking for wealth, long life, or the death of his enemies, he asked for wisdom. God honored his request, granting him exceptional wisdom and insight.

Verse Reference:

"Give your servant, therefore, an understanding heart to judge your people, that I may discern between good and bad: for who is able to judge this thy so great a people?" — 1 Kings 3:9

Expository Insight:

The Hebrew word for "understanding" (shama, שָׁמַע, Strong's H8085) also means "hearing." Solomon's request for an understanding or "hearing" heart signifies his desire for wisdom that listens deeply—to God, to the people, and to the situations he would face. His wisdom was founded on humility and a deep desire to serve justly.

Theological Implication:

Solomon's request for wisdom highlights an important spiritual principle: wisdom begins with humility and a desire to serve others. Solomon's example encourages us to seek wisdom not for self-promotion or personal gain but to understand and help others.

2. The Case of the Two Mothers and the Baby

One of the most famous examples of Solomon's wisdom is the story of the two women who claimed to be the mother of the same baby (1 Kings 3:16-28). This story is often cited as a powerful example of discernment, demonstrating Solomon's ability to see beyond words and actions to the heart of the matter.

Story Summary:

Two women came before Solomon, each claiming to be the mother of a baby. Solomon proposed to cut the baby in two so each woman would receive half. One woman agreed to this, but the other, who was the real mother, pleaded to give the child to the other woman to spare the baby's life. Through this display of compassion, Solomon recognized the true mother.

Verse Reference:

"Then the king answered and said, Give her the living child, and in no wise slay it: she is the mother thereof." — 1 Kings 3:27

Expository Insight:

The wisdom here lies in Solomon's understanding of human nature. He knew that the true mother's love would reveal itself in her willingness to sacrifice her claim to save her child. The term "Solomonic wisdom" has since become synonymous with insight and fairness, especially in difficult or seemingly unsolvable situations.

Theological Implication:

This story demonstrates the divine nature of true wisdom. God's wisdom discerns the heart, distinguishing truth from deception. This example encourages us to seek God's guidance in situations that seem impossible to solve, trusting that His wisdom can reveal the truth and bring justice.

3. Solomon's Insight into Nature and Creation

Solomon's wisdom extended beyond human relationships and justice; he had remarkable insight into nature, science, and the created order. In 1 Kings 4:33, we read that Solomon spoke of trees, animals, birds, and fish.

This depth of understanding made him a revered figure not only for his governance but also for his intellectual and scientific contributions.

Verse Reference:

"And he spake of trees, from the cedar tree that is in Lebanon even unto the hyssop that springeth out of the wall: he spake also of beasts, and of fowl, and of creeping things, and of fishes." — 1 Kings 4:33

Expository Insight:

The Hebrew word for "spoke" (dabar, דָּבַר, Strong's H1696) implies not just casual conversation but an organized, thoughtful discourse. Solomon's knowledge was comprehensive, from large, impressive trees like the cedars of Lebanon to humble plants like hyssop. His understanding reflected an awareness of God's intricate design in all aspects of creation.

Theological Implication:

This profound understanding of nature illustrates that wisdom encompasses a reverence for all of God's creation. Solomon's wisdom shows that to know God deeply is also to appreciate His handiwork in the natural world. As Psalm

111:2 states, "Great are the works of the Lord, studied by all who delight in them."

4. Solomon's Wisdom in Governance and Building the Temple

Another example of Solomon's wisdom is his role in building the Temple, a complex and monumental project that required not only architectural knowledge but also spiritual discernment and a clear understanding of worship. Solomon gathered resources, engaged skilled laborers, and followed God's instructions to build a house for His name.

Verse Reference:

"Then Solomon began to build the house of the Lord at Jerusalem in mount Moriah, where the Lord appeared unto David his father." — 2 Chronicles 3:1

Expository Insight:

The Hebrew word for "house" (bayith, בַּיִת, Strong's H1004) signifies not only a dwelling but a sanctuary, a place set apart for God. Solomon's wisdom in organizing and executing this project reflects a deep understanding of God's holiness and the importance of proper worship.

Theological Implication:

The building of the Temple underscores the idea that true wisdom involves knowing God's priorities. Solomon's wisdom enabled him to create a space that would draw people closer to God. This teaches us that wisdom involves aligning our actions with God's purposes, prioritizing what honors Him over personal ambition.

5. Solomon's Counsel on the Value of Wisdom

Solomon's writings in Proverbs reflect his teachings on wisdom. His counsel on wisdom's value, especially in contrast to material wealth, remains as relevant today as it was in ancient times. Solomon understood that wisdom was a greater asset than any amount of wealth or possessions.

Verse Reference:

"How much better to get wisdom than gold, and good judgment than silver!" — Proverbs 16:16

Expository Insight:

The Hebrew word for "wisdom" here is chokmah, which conveys the sense of skill and expertise applied in practical situations. The word for "good judgment" (biynah, בִּינָה, Strong's H998) implies discernment and understanding, qualities that go beyond mere intellect.

Theological Implication:

Solomon's teachings remind us that wisdom is invaluable in our lives. While material wealth may offer comfort, only wisdom provides guidance for moral, spiritual, and relational challenges. Seeking wisdom is an acknowledgment that life's greatest treasures are found in our relationship with God and our understanding of His ways.

6. Solomon's Downfall and the Limits of Human Wisdom

While Solomon's wisdom was great, his life serves as a cautionary tale. Despite his wisdom, Solomon's heart eventually turned away from God, leading him to make unwise choices influenced by foreign alliances and idolatry. This turning point highlights the limits of human wisdom without a strong foundation in faithfulness to God.

Verse Reference:

"For when Solomon was old, his wives turned away his heart after other gods: and his heart was not perfect with the Lord his God." — 1 Kings 11:4

Expository Insight:

The Hebrew term for "heart" (leb, לֵב, Strong's H3820) denotes not only emotions but also the mind and will. Solomon's heart, initially devoted to God, became divided. This shift illustrates that wisdom, if not grounded in unwavering faithfulness to God, can lead to ruin.

Theological Implication:

Solomon's story reminds us that wisdom must be paired with obedience and devotion to God. True wisdom acknowledges human limitations and remains reliant on God. Even the wisest among us are susceptible to error if we stray from God's ways, emphasizing the importance of humility and a heart devoted to Him.

The life and wisdom of Solomon provide profound lessons about discernment, justice, and humility. Through his actions, writings, and decisions, Solomon demonstrated that wisdom is more than knowledge; it is a God-given ability to understand and apply truth in ways that honor God. However, his life also serves as a reminder of the limits of human wisdom without obedience to God. Solomonic wisdom calls us to seek discernment, pursue justice, and anchor ourselves in a faithful relationship with God, knowing that true wisdom ultimately comes from Him.

Wisdom as a Gift of the Holy Spirit

In the Bible, wisdom is described as a divine gift that grants individuals the ability to perceive the world through God's eyes, recognize His truth, and apply that truth to bring Him glory. Unlike human knowledge, which is limited and often biased, the wisdom given by the Holy Spirit offers insight aligned with God's purposes and will. This chapter explores wisdom as a supernatural gift, given by God to those who seek Him, enabling them to navigate life's complexities in a way that honors Him.

The Nature of Wisdom as a Divine Gift

The Bible tells us that wisdom is not merely intellectual knowledge or practical know-how; it is a spiritual insight that allows us to discern God's will and see things from His perspective. Wisdom is described as one of the seven gifts of the Holy Spirit in the New Testament, as seen in 1 Corinthians 12:8 and in the Old Testament as a divine attribute, particularly in the books of Proverbs and Isaiah.

Verse Reference:

"For to one is given by the Spirit the word of wisdom; to another the word of knowledge by the same Spirit." — 1 Corinthians 12:8

Expository Insight:

The Greek word for "wisdom" here is sophia (σοφία, Strong's G4678), which implies insight into divine things, understanding that goes beyond human reasoning, and the ability to make decisions in alignment with God's truth. This wisdom differs from earthly wisdom, as noted in James 3:17, where it is described as "pure, peaceable, gentle, open to reason, full of mercy and good fruits."

Theological Implication:

The spiritual gift of wisdom enables believers to interpret and apply God's truth to their lives and the lives of others. It's a way of knowing that surpasses intellectual comprehension and is deeply connected to spiritual discernment.

1. The Role of the Holy Spirit in Granting Wisdom

The Holy Spirit is the source of divine wisdom, actively working within believers to grant them insight, understanding, and the ability to discern truth. In the book of Isaiah, the Messiah is prophesied to be filled with the "Spirit of wisdom and understanding."

Verse Reference:

"And the spirit of the Lord shall rest upon him, the spirit of wisdom and understanding, the spirit of counsel and might, the spirit of knowledge and of the fear of the Lord."
— Isaiah 11:2

Expository Insight:

The Hebrew term for "wisdom" here is chokmah (חָכְמָה, Strong's H2451), referring to a skillful and wise heart, one that is skilled in understanding and application. Chokmah is not limited to intellectual insight; it is practical wisdom that brings God's ways to bear on everyday life.

Theological Implication:

Isaiah's prophecy of the Spirit of wisdom resting on the Messiah shows that wisdom is fundamentally rooted in one's relationship with God. Just as Christ was filled with wisdom, believers too are called to live by the wisdom given through the Holy Spirit, reflecting God's character in their actions and decisions.

2. Understanding Truth from God's Perspective

True wisdom involves recognizing and adhering to the truths of God. In John 16:13, Jesus says that the Spirit will guide us into all truth. This truth goes beyond surface-level understanding; it enables believers to see situations and people as God does, with compassion, clarity, and righteousness.

Verse Reference:

"Howbeit when he, the Spirit of truth, is come, he will guide you into all truth: for he shall not speak of himself; but whatsoever he shall hear, that shall he speak: and he will shew you things to come." — John 16:13

Expository Insight:

The Greek word for "truth" is aletheia (ἀλήθεια, Strong's G225), signifying not just factual correctness but the reality aligned with God's perspective. The Holy Spirit's role as the "Spirit of truth" emphasizes His function in leading believers into a deeper, more authentic understanding of God's ways.

Theological Implication:

This guiding into truth means that the wisdom given by the Holy Spirit is always grounded in God's nature and will. It assures believers that wisdom is not subjective but a reflection of God's absolute truth, which leads them to make choices that honor Him.

3. Wisdom as an Instrument to Glorify God

A key aspect of the wisdom granted by the Holy Spirit is that it brings glory to God. As believers live out the wisdom they receive, they reflect God's goodness and draw others closer to Him. This wisdom impacts relationships, decisions, and actions, all of which can serve to demonstrate God's character to the world.

Verse Reference:

"But the wisdom that is from above is first pure, then peaceable, gentle, and easy to be entreated, full of mercy and good fruits, without partiality, and without hypocrisy." — James 3:17

Expository Insight:

The Greek word for "pure" is hagnos (ἁγνός, Strong's G53), meaning undefiled or holy. The term "peaceable" (eirēnikos, εἰρηνικός, Strong's G1516) suggests a wisdom that fosters harmony and well-being. This purity and peaceability reveal that divine wisdom is fundamentally different from worldly wisdom, characterized by integrity, gentleness, and a commitment to God's purposes.

Theological Implication:

Divine wisdom brings glory to God because it embodies His nature. When believers act with wisdom, they reflect attributes that come directly from Him—holiness, peace, and compassion—ultimately pointing back to God's glory and His work within them.

4. Applying Wisdom in Practical Decision-Making

The wisdom given by the Holy Spirit is intensely practical. It impacts how we approach daily decisions, discernment in relationships, and the challenges we face. Proverbs 3:5-6 calls believers to trust in the Lord and lean not on their own understanding, showing that true wisdom is often about surrendering our perspectives for God's.

Verse Reference:

"Trust in the Lord with all thine heart; and lean not unto thine own understanding. In all thy ways acknowledge him, and he shall direct thy paths." — Proverbs 3:5-6

Expository Insight:

The Hebrew word for "trust" is batach (בָּטַח, Strong's H982), meaning to rely on with confidence. To "lean" on God means to rely on Him rather than our limited insight. This calls believers to a position of humility, acknowledging that God's wisdom surpasses human understanding.

Theological Implication:

This passage emphasizes the relational nature of wisdom. Relying on God's wisdom over our own understanding is a testament to our faith and trust in His character. It teaches believers that divine wisdom requires us to actively submit our will to God, allowing Him to guide our paths.

5. Wisdom as a Source of Strength and Peace

The wisdom that comes from the Holy Spirit brings inner strength, peace, and resilience, qualities needed for navigating the trials of life. In Isaiah 33:6, wisdom is described as the stability of times, showing that God-given wisdom provides a firm foundation.

Verse Reference:

"And wisdom and knowledge shall be the stability of thy times, and strength of salvation: the fear of the Lord is his treasure." — Isaiah 33:6

Expository Insight:

The Hebrew word for "stability" (emunah, אֱמוּנָה, Strong's H530) is associated with firmness, faithfulness, and truth. Wisdom provides a steady, reliable foundation, reflecting the unchanging nature of God Himself.

Theological Implication:

This insight shows that wisdom not only provides insight but also anchors the soul. As believers grow in wisdom, they find strength and security, understanding that God's truth is unchanging and reliable. Wisdom becomes a source of peace, empowering believers to face uncertainty with confidence.

Wisdom, as a gift of the Holy Spirit, offers a unique perspective that aligns with God's truth, guiding believers in a life that brings glory to Him. From seeing truth as God sees it, to applying it in practical decisions, this wisdom impacts every area of life. Wisdom is a divine invitation to know God's heart and live in a way that reflects His glory, peace, and stability. By seeking and embracing this gift, believers fulfill their calling to walk in the ways of the Lord, trusting that His wisdom will guide, strengthen, and sustain them.

CHAPTER 04

THE FEAR OF THE LORD IS WISDOM

The Bible repeatedly asserts that "the fear of the Lord is the beginning of wisdom" (Proverbs 9:10). In Proverbs 8:13, wisdom is personified, declaring, "To fear the Lord is to hate evil; I hate pride and arrogance, evil behavior and perverse speech." This chapter seeks to unfold the true meaning of "fearing the Lord," exploring how this reverence initiates true wisdom and transforms our lives.

Understanding the "Fear of the Lord"

The term "fear of the Lord" might sound intimidating, yet in the context of biblical wisdom, it doesn't mean to live in terror. Instead, it conveys a deep sense of respect, reverence, and awe for God's majesty, righteousness, and authority. In Hebrew, the word for "fear" is yirah (יְרְאָה, Strong's H3374), which denotes respect and worshipful submission. This kind of "fear" is the foundation upon which true wisdom is built.

Verse Reference:

"The fear of the Lord is the beginning of knowledge; fools despise wisdom and instruction." — Proverbs 1:7

Expository Insight:

Here, "beginning" translates from the Hebrew reshith (רֵאשִׁית, Strong's H7225), indicating not just a starting point but the principal or foundational element. Thus, "the fear of the Lord" is essential to acquiring wisdom—it shapes our understanding of all things.

Theological Implication:

The fear of the Lord draws us into alignment with God's character and His standards of holiness. This reverence helps us recognize that God's ways are supreme, leading us to humbly submit and seek wisdom from Him, rather than relying on human reasoning alone.

1. The Connection Between Fear of the Lord and Hatred of Evil

According to Proverbs 8:13, the fear of the Lord leads to a disdain for evil, pride, arrogance, and corruption. This hatred of evil is not mere avoidance of wrongdoing but a proactive rejection of anything that stands against God's nature.

Verse Reference:

"To fear the Lord is to hate evil; I hate pride and arrogance, evil behavior and perverse speech." — Proverbs 8:13

Expository Insight:

The Hebrew word for "hate" here is sane (שָׂנֵא, Strong's H8130), meaning to detest or reject completely. True wisdom doesn't allow for neutrality toward evil; it fosters an active disdain for what contradicts God's holiness.

Theological Implication:

This verse emphasizes that genuine wisdom involves a moral stance aligned with God's righteousness. Fear of the Lord compels us to reject pride (ga'on, Strong's H1347) and arrogance (zadown, Strong's H2087), attitudes that exalt self over God. As believers, we are called to despise sin, understanding that our love for God and pursuit of wisdom must lead us to embrace purity and integrity.

2. The Fear of the Lord as a Path to Life

The Bible repeatedly associates the fear of the Lord with life, fulfillment, and safety. Far from bringing dread, this reverence for God offers us guidance, blessing, and protection.

Verse Reference:

"The fear of the Lord leads to life, so that one may sleep satisfied, untouched by evil." — Proverbs 19:23

Expository Insight:

The Hebrew word for "life" here is chay (חי, Strong's H2416), which signifies more than physical existence. It implies fullness, well-being, and a life lived in God's favor. The fear of the Lord provides a secure foundation, leading to peace and satisfaction.

Theological Implication:

This verse illustrates that fearing God means living under His guidance, which leads to a fulfilling life. A life marked by wisdom is grounded in a fear of the Lord that brings rest from spiritual conflict, freedom from sin's grip, and assurance in God's protection.

3. Reverence as an Expression of Trust

To fear the Lord also means to trust Him deeply. Reverence is not only about honoring God's majesty but about submitting to His guidance and trusting His goodness, even when we do not fully understand His ways.

Verse Reference:

"Trust in the Lord with all your heart, and lean not on your own understanding." — Proverbs 3:5

Expository Insight:

The Hebrew word for "trust" here is batach (בָּטַח, Strong's H982), which suggests reliance and confidence. It conveys a commitment to entrust ourselves to God completely, putting aside our limited perspectives.

Theological Implication:

Trust is central to the fear of the Lord. Reverence for God naturally flows into a reliance on Him. As we trust in Him wholeheartedly, we recognize His wisdom and goodness as surpassing our own, leading us to seek His ways over our own understanding.

4. The Fear of the Lord as a Guide to Wisdom and Discernment

Reverence for God shapes our decisions and enhances our discernment. Wisdom in decision-making flows from a life aligned with God's standards, and the fear of the Lord sets that foundation.

Verse Reference:

"The fear of the Lord is the beginning of wisdom; a good understanding have all they that do his commandments." — Psalm 111:10

Expository Insight:

The Hebrew word tov (טוֹב, Strong's H2896) here means "good," emphasizing that wisdom aligned with God's commandments is wholesome, beneficial, and inherently good. This form of wisdom influences our conduct, leading us to live in accordance with God's will.

Theological Implication:

Wisdom rooted in the fear of the Lord influences both thought and behavior. By recognizing God's holiness and authority, we cultivate a sense of discernment that guides us away from sin and aligns us with His righteousness. This discernment enables believers to navigate complex situations with integrity and godliness.

5. Fearing the Lord and Rejecting Pride

The fear of the Lord inherently leads to humility. Recognizing God's greatness and wisdom brings us into a position of humility, rejecting pride and self-centeredness.

Verse Reference:

"Before destruction the heart of man is haughty, and before honor is humility." — Proverbs 18:12

Expository Insight:

The Hebrew word for "haughty" is gobah (גָּבַהּ, Strong's H1363), indicating a proud and arrogant attitude. In contrast, "humility" is shaphal (שָׁפָל, Strong's H8217), meaning lowliness or modesty. Wisdom drives us away from the arrogance that leads to downfall and toward the humility that honors God.

Theological Implication:

True wisdom, rooted in the fear of the Lord, produces humility. When we understand God's holiness, we are less likely to exalt ourselves. Instead, wisdom moves us to act with humility, knowing that every good thing comes from God.

Practical Application: Living with Reverence

Fearing the Lord is not merely about reverence but about a daily commitment to live under His lordship. When we truly fear God, we align our lives with His Word, submitting our plans, choices, and desires to Him.

Verse Reference:

"Let us hear the conclusion of the whole matter: Fear God, and keep his commandments: for this is the whole duty of man." — Ecclesiastes 12:13

Expository Insight:

The Hebrew word for "duty" is kol (כֹּל, Strong's H3605), meaning "all" or "everything." It emphasizes that reverence for God and obedience to His commands is the essence of a life well-lived.

Theological Implication:

Fearing the Lord is the foundation for a life that pleases God. It calls us to live with a clear purpose: to honor God in all that we do. This reverence influences our thoughts, words, and actions, enabling us to pursue holiness and reject anything contrary to His character.

Reverence as the Foundation of Wisdom

The fear of the Lord is more than a feeling of respect; it is the very foundation of a life lived in alignment with God's will. This reverence produces a wisdom that hates evil, rejects pride, and walks in humility. By fearing the Lord, we recognize His authority and submit ourselves to His guidance, enabling us to live lives that glorify Him.

The wisdom that comes from fearing the Lord is a gift, and it requires us to put aside our pride and ego, seeking instead to understand and honor God's will above all else. True wisdom calls us to walk humbly with our Creator, allowing His Word to shape our lives and guide our paths.

The Fear of the Lord is the Beginning of Wisdom

Key Verse

"The fear of the Lord is the beginning of wisdom, and the knowledge of the Holy One is insight." — Proverbs 9:10

The idea that "the fear of the Lord is the beginning of wisdom" is repeated throughout the Bible, especially in the books of Proverbs and Psalms. This phrase can be challenging to understand, especially in modern times, where "fear" often implies dread or terror. However, in biblical terms, the "fear of the Lord" refers to a reverential awe and deep respect for God's holiness, justice, and majesty. This reverence becomes the foundation upon which true wisdom is built. In this chapter, we'll explore how the fear of God is not just the starting point of wisdom but also a crucial lens through which we view and understand life itself.

1. Understanding the Fear of the Lord: A Foundation for Wisdom

In the Hebrew text, the word "fear" is yirah (יִרְאָה, Strong's H3374), which conveys a sense of reverence, awe, and respect. The concept goes beyond mere obedience; it includes a deep awareness of God's nature, His sovereignty, and His justice. Recognizing the greatness and holiness of God forms the foundation upon which we build our understanding of everything else.

Verse Reference:

"The fear of the Lord is the beginning of knowledge; fools despise wisdom and instruction." — Proverbs 1:7

Expository Insight:

The Hebrew term for "beginning" here is reshith (רֵאשִׁית, Strong's H7225), meaning the starting point or principal element. The phrase suggests that wisdom doesn't truly begin until one understands and respects God's authority. Wisdom built on any other foundation lacks depth and fails to guide us toward eternal truths.

Theological Implication:

This reverential fear establishes wisdom in God's character rather than human understanding. It is not merely the first step but the essential starting point that shapes our entire pursuit of knowledge, morality, and purpose.

2. The Intrinsic Nature of Wisdom as God's Attribute

Wisdom is an essential and eternal attribute of God. As revealed in Scripture, wisdom is part of God's very nature, and His creation reflects His wisdom. In Proverbs 8, wisdom is personified and speaks as a witness to God's acts in creation, showing that wisdom was present "before His deeds of old" (Proverbs 8:22-23). This passage implies that wisdom is intrinsically bound to God's being.

Verse Reference:

"For the Lord gives wisdom; from his mouth come knowledge and understanding." — Proverbs 2:6

Expository Insight:

The Hebrew word for "wisdom" here is chokmah (חָכְמָה, Strong's H2451), which signifies skill, knowledge, and discernment. God is the source of all true wisdom, and His wisdom is given to those who fear Him.

Theological Implication:

If wisdom is an intrinsic attribute of God, then fearing the Lord doesn't just lead to wisdom; it brings us into alignment with His very nature. Reverence for God allows us to participate in His wisdom, which transcends human limitations and gives us insight that only He can provide.

3. Reverence as a Path to Moral Discernment

The fear of the Lord brings clarity to our moral compass, guiding us toward what is right and away from what is wrong. It teaches us to hate evil, pride, and arrogance—all things that God despises (Proverbs 8:13). A reverential fear of God instills in us a hatred for sin, not because of fear of punishment but out of respect for God's holiness.

Verse Reference:

"To fear the Lord is to hate evil; I hate pride and arrogance, evil behavior and perverse speech." — Proverbs 8:13

Expository Insight:

The term "hate" in this context is sane (שָׂנֵא, Strong's H8130), which means to utterly reject. Fearing God leads to a rejection of sin and anything that contradicts His nature. This hate for evil becomes part of the moral fabric of a believer's life.

Theological Implication:

The fear of the Lord reshapes our moral decisions, making us sensitive to sin and aware of God's standards. True wisdom doesn't only guide us in practical matters but deeply influences our ethical beliefs, helping us align with God's heart and will.

4. Reverence for God as Trust in His Wisdom

Fearing the Lord includes recognizing that His wisdom far exceeds our own. To fear God is to trust Him completely, knowing that His understanding surpasses ours. This trust redirects us from relying on our limited perspective to seeking His guidance in all aspects of life.

Verse Reference:

"Trust in the Lord with all your heart, and do not lean on your own understanding." — Proverbs 3:5

Expository Insight:

The Hebrew word for "trust" is batach (בָּטַח, Strong's H982), meaning to have confidence in or rely on. By trusting in the Lord, we acknowledge His supreme wisdom and allow His understanding to guide our lives.

Theological Implication:

Trust is a vital expression of the fear of the Lord. When we recognize God's authority and wisdom, we are freed from the limitations of our understanding. This trust is not passive; it actively shapes our thoughts, decisions, and actions, grounding them in God's character rather than human reasoning.

5. How Reverence Leads to Humility

A key outcome of fearing the Lord is humility. Recognizing God's greatness puts our own knowledge and abilities into perspective, humbling us and removing pride. Proverbs contrasts humility with the pride that leads to destruction (Proverbs 16:18). To fear God is to submit to His authority, acknowledging that we are finite and dependent on His guidance.

Verse Reference:

"Before a downfall the heart is haughty, but humility comes before honor." — Proverbs 18:12

Expository Insight:

The Hebrew term for "humility" is shaphal (שָׁפָל, Strong's H8217), which denotes lowliness or modesty. Wisdom begins when we are humble enough to recognize our limitations and acknowledge God's wisdom.

Theological Implication:

Humility born out of reverence for God keeps us grounded in His truths and prevents us from the arrogance that leads to moral failure. By surrendering our pride, we allow God's wisdom to elevate our understanding and grant us insight beyond our own.

6. The Fear of the Lord as a Guiding Light

Living in reverence toward God provides a steady compass that guides our lives, illuminating our path in a world full of uncertainty and challenges. Wisdom, rooted in the fear of the Lord, is not just about acquiring knowledge but about walking in the light of His guidance.

Verse Reference:

"Your word is a lamp to my feet and a light to my path." — Psalm 119:105

Expository Insight:

In this context, the Hebrew word for "light" is or (אוֹר, Strong's H216), which signifies illumination and guidance. God's wisdom is the light that leads us through life's choices, showing us the right path.

Theological Implication:

The fear of the Lord, grounded in His Word, shines as a guiding light that reveals the righteous path. It's not simply about obeying rules; it's about having a relationship with the Source of all wisdom, whose light leads us through life's darkness.

Embracing the Fear of the Lord

The fear of the Lord is the foundation of wisdom, guiding our decisions, shaping our moral compass, and illuminating our lives. This reverence allows us to partake in God's wisdom, aligning our hearts with His character and helping us live in harmony with His ways. Embracing the fear of the Lord is the beginning of wisdom—not as an intellectual pursuit, but as a lived reality that touches every part of our lives. When we honor God with reverence and awe, we find ourselves growing in wisdom, strength, and purpose.

Final Reflection

Embracing the fear of the Lord is more than reverence; it is the acknowledgment of God's authority, holiness, and love for His creation. When we approach life with this profound respect for God, we open ourselves to the vast treasures of wisdom He freely offers to those who seek Him.

CHAPTER 05

WISDOM IN CREATION

Key Verse

"I was there when he set the heavens in place, when he marked out the horizon on the face of the deep." — Proverbs 8:27

In Proverbs 8, Wisdom is personified and depicted as an active presence during the creation of the world. This portrayal emphasizes that wisdom is foundational to the order, beauty, and intricacy of the universe. Wisdom, often seen as an abstract quality, is here shown to be a tangible reality interwoven with creation itself, manifesting through the laws of nature, the complexity of life, and the harmony of all created things. By exploring the wisdom embedded in creation, we see God's intentionality and purpose for His creation, revealing His character and inviting us to live in harmony with His design.

1. Wisdom's Presence from the Beginning

The concept of wisdom existing before creation speaks to its foundational role in God's plan. Wisdom is not something developed over time; rather, it is an intrinsic attribute of God that was present from the beginning. Proverbs 8:22-23 declares, "The Lord brought me forth as the first of his works, before his deeds of old; I was formed long ages ago, at the very beginning, when the world came to be."

Verse Reference:

"In the beginning, God created the heavens and the earth." — Genesis 1:1

Expository Insight:

In Genesis, the word "beginning" is reshith (רֵאשִׁית, Strong's H7225), which is also the root word used in Proverbs 8:22. This parallel suggests that wisdom was not only present but instrumental in God's creative work. Before the heavens and earth, wisdom was established as the guiding principle.

Theological Implication:

Wisdom is eternal, part of God's divine nature, and thus essential to all of creation. Recognizing this shows that wisdom is not merely knowledge but a divine order that flows directly from God Himself. This understanding gives creation an intentional purpose, aligning it with God's perfect wisdom.

2. The Role of Wisdom as Creator's Architect

Proverbs 8:27-30 illustrates Wisdom as actively involved in forming the world, stating, "I was there when he set the heavens in place, when he marked out the horizon on the face of the deep… Then I was constantly at his side. I was filled with delight day after day, rejoicing always in his presence."

Verse Reference:

"The heavens declare the glory of God; the skies proclaim the work of his hands." — Psalm 19:1

Expository Insight:

The word "declare" in Hebrew is saphar (סָפַר, Strong's H5608), meaning to recount or announce. The very structure of the universe reveals the wisdom with which it was created, pointing to God's glory and intelligence. Every detail of creation, from the laws governing the planets to the intricacies of ecosystems, is an expression of divine wisdom.

Theological Implication:

Creation itself is a testimony to God's wisdom. The heavens, earth, and every form of life are not random occurrences but carefully crafted manifestations of divine wisdom. Recognizing wisdom as the architect of creation encourages us to respect and value all aspects of the natural world, seeing them as expressions of God's intentional design.

3. The Order and Harmony in Creation as Evidence of Wisdom

The concept of order in creation reveals God's wisdom in the design of natural laws and the harmony within ecosystems. Proverbs 8:29 states, "when he gave the sea its boundary so the waters would not overstep his command, and when he marked out the foundations of the earth." Here, wisdom is portrayed as setting boundaries and establishing order.

Verse Reference:

"He has made everything beautiful in its time. He has also set eternity in the human heart." — Ecclesiastes 3:11

Expository Insight:

The word "beautiful" is yapheh (יָפֶה, Strong's H3303), which can also mean well-ordered or fitting. This verse aligns with the idea that creation's beauty is found in its order and purpose. God's wisdom is visible in how every element in creation has its place and time, contributing to an overall harmony.

Theological Implication:

God's wisdom provides a template for living harmoniously with creation. The order and boundaries God established teach us that wisdom respects structure and boundaries, aligning our lives with God's intended design. This understanding fosters humility and responsibility in how we interact with the world, valuing the balance and purpose in all creation.

4. The Complexity of Life as a Manifestation of Wisdom

The complexity of life—from the structure of a single cell to the human body—is a profound demonstration of God's wisdom. Proverbs 8 implies that wisdom is woven into the very fabric of life itself. Every organism functions within a complex and precise system, displaying God's intricate design.

Verse Reference:

"For you created my inmost being; you knit me together in my mother's womb." — Psalm 139:13

Expository Insight:

The Hebrew word "knit" is sakhak (סָכַך, Strong's H5526), which conveys intricate weaving or covering. The psalmist acknowledges God's hand in forming every part of the human body, underscoring the complexity and care involved in creation. This complexity reveals God's wisdom and His intimate knowledge of creation.

Theological Implication:

Wisdom in creation is not only grand but also profoundly personal. Understanding that God's wisdom is involved in every aspect of our being brings a sense of purpose and value to each individual life. We are part of a divine design, and recognizing this allows us to honor our bodies and lives as gifts from a wise Creator.

5. Creation's Testimony to Divine Wisdom

Creation itself bears witness to God's wisdom, serving as a source of revelation to humanity. Romans 1:20 states that "since the creation of the world God's invisible qualities—his eternal power and divine nature—have been clearly seen, being understood from what has been made."

Verse Reference:

"When I consider your heavens, the work of your fingers, the moon and the stars, which you have set in place…" — Psalm 8:3

Expository Insight:

The phrase "work of your fingers" is a poetic expression emphasizing God's deliberate and detailed craftsmanship. Every star, planet, and constellation reflects God's wisdom, showcasing His power and attention to detail.

Theological Implication:

Nature itself is a form of divine revelation, pointing us toward God's wisdom and encouraging us to seek Him. Creation's testimony challenges us to recognize God's existence and His attributes, calling us to live in reverence and gratitude. By observing nature, we gain insights into God's character and are drawn closer to Him.

6. Humanity's Role in Reflecting Wisdom in Creation

Since humanity is made in God's image, we are also called to reflect His wisdom. In Genesis, God commands humanity to "fill the earth and subdue it" (Genesis 1:28). This command is a call to steward creation wisely, aligning our actions with the wisdom God has built into the world.

Verse Reference:

"The fear of the Lord—that is wisdom, and to shun evil is understanding." — Job 28:28

Expository Insight:

The Hebrew word for "shun" here is suwr (סור, Strong's H5493), meaning to turn away. By respecting God's wisdom, we honor our role as caretakers of creation, avoiding actions that harm the world and acting in ways that align with God's design.

Theological Implication:

Our reverence for God's wisdom calls us to be responsible stewards of His creation. By acknowledging that creation reflects God's wisdom, we are reminded of our duty to protect and care for it. This responsibility extends to every area of life, encouraging us to live in harmony with God's order.

Wisdom in Creation as an Invitation to Worship

God's wisdom is evident in every part of creation, from the stars in the sky to the smallest organism. Wisdom was present from the beginning, a guiding principle that shaped the universe. Recognizing wisdom in creation invites us into a deeper relationship with God, as we see His intentionality, care, and beauty reflected in the world around us.

Verse Reflection:

"Great are the works of the Lord; they are pondered by all who delight in them." — Psalm 111:2

The beauty and order of creation inspire us to worship and to seek wisdom ourselves. As we consider the wisdom of God in the world around us, we are encouraged to align our lives with His principles, to care for His creation, and to live in reverence and awe of His eternal wisdom.

The Personification of Wisdom – Is Wisdom God?

Key Verse

"I was there when he set the heavens in place, when he marked out the horizon on the face of the deep." — Proverbs 8:27

In Proverbs 8, wisdom is personified as a woman, speaking in the first person ("I was there…") and describing her presence at the very foundation of creation. This personification is striking, suggesting that wisdom is more than just a concept; it seems to embody a divine quality that predates creation itself. But why is wisdom depicted as female? And does the language used here suggest that wisdom is an aspect of God Himself, or perhaps a reference to Jesus, often identified as the divine "Word" in the New Testament? In this chapter, we will explore these profound questions and seek to understand the relationship between wisdom, God, and Christ, using the Bible and concordance tools for deeper insights.

1. The Personification of Wisdom as Female

Throughout the book of Proverbs, wisdom is personified as a female figure. Proverbs 8:1-3 introduces her as "Lady Wisdom," calling out to humanity from public places. But why is wisdom given a female voice?

Verse Reference:

"Does not wisdom call out? Does not understanding raise her voice?" — Proverbs 8:1

Expository Insight:

In Hebrew, the word for wisdom (chokmah, חָכְמָה, Strong's H2451) is a feminine noun. Ancient Hebrew culture often used gendered language to communicate complex ideas, and the personification of abstract qualities was common. By giving wisdom a feminine form, the text emphasizes relational and nurturing aspects, which complements wisdom's role as a guide, protector, and advocate for humanity's best interests.

Theological Implication:

The female personification of wisdom highlights her compassionate, guiding nature. Just as a nurturing figure would call out to lead and protect, Lady Wisdom appeals to humanity to follow God's ways. This depiction also aligns with the nurturing qualities attributed to wisdom, helping us see it not only as intellectual knowledge but as a force that seeks humanity's well-being.

2. The "I" in Wisdom's Speech: Is Wisdom Divine?

Proverbs 8:27 describes wisdom using the pronoun "I," creating the impression that wisdom has a personal, active presence. This language raises the question of whether wisdom is merely a poetic device or if it has a divine nature.

Verse Reference:

"The Lord brought me forth as the first of his works, before his deeds of old." — Proverbs 8:22

Expository Insight:

The phrase "brought me forth" is translated from the Hebrew qanah (קָנָה, Strong's H7069), which can mean "to create," "to possess," or "to acquire." This phrasing has been debated, as it suggests that wisdom was a fundamental part of God's creative activity, yet distinct from God Himself. Wisdom speaks of being "brought forth," yet also being integral to God's work.

Theological Implication:

The use of "I" here may indicate that wisdom, while not a separate deity, is an expression of God's nature. Wisdom exists in relationship to God, embodying His intellect, order, and purpose. Rather than viewing wisdom as an independent being, we can understand it as God's rational presence, intertwined with creation and actively involved in the world.

3. Wisdom and the Logos: Is Wisdom a Prefiguration of Christ?

In the New Testament, Jesus is described as the "Word" (Greek: Logos, Λόγος), the divine agent of creation. John 1:1-3 states, "In the beginning was the Word, and the Word was with God, and the Word was God… Through him all things were made." This language closely parallels Proverbs 8, leading many to wonder if wisdom in Proverbs 8 foreshadows Christ.

Verse Reference:

"In the beginning was the Word, and the Word was with God, and the Word was God." — John 1:1

Expository Insight:

The Greek term Logos (Strong's G3056) means "word," "reason," or "principle." It is a concept that denotes the active, creative force of God. By identifying Christ as the Logos, John's Gospel reveals Jesus as the wisdom through whom all things were made. Just as Proverbs describes wisdom as a participant in creation, John describes Christ as integral to the act of creation.

Theological Implication:

If wisdom in Proverbs 8 prefigures Christ, then wisdom is indeed a part of God's eternal nature, manifested in Jesus. This understanding gives us a Christological lens through which we view wisdom: wisdom is not only a quality of God but also embodied fully in Christ. By connecting wisdom with Jesus, we see wisdom as a divine, active force that brings creation into alignment with God's character.

4. Wisdom's Role in Creation and God's Intrinsic Attributes

Proverbs 8 emphasizes that wisdom was present at the creation of the world, suggesting that wisdom is an intrinsic attribute of God, much like His holiness or love.

Verse Reference:

"The fear of the Lord is the beginning of wisdom, and knowledge of the Holy One is understanding." — Proverbs 9:10

Expository Insight:

The phrase "fear of the Lord" here uses the Hebrew word yirah (יִרְאָה, Strong's H3374), which implies reverence and awe. This reverence initiates wisdom because it aligns us with God's perspective, allowing His attributes, such as wisdom, to be understood as reflections of His holiness.

Theological Implication:

Wisdom, then, is a reflection of God's eternal attributes. It's not a separate being or entity but is woven into the essence of God Himself. When we seek wisdom, we are seeking an understanding of God's own nature. God's wisdom is boundless and eternal, revealing the order, purpose, and beauty within creation, aligning all things to reflect His glory.

5. The Practical Application of Divine Wisdom

By understanding wisdom as both a part of God's nature and embodied in Christ, we gain insights into how to apply wisdom practically. Divine wisdom is not only for contemplation but for action, directing us toward righteous and godly living.

Verse Reference:

"But the wisdom that comes from heaven is first of all pure; then peace-loving, considerate, submissive, full of mercy and good fruit, impartial and sincere." — James 3:17

Expository Insight:

James's description of heavenly wisdom aligns with the qualities of wisdom seen in Proverbs. The Greek word for "wisdom" here is sophia (σοφία, Strong's G4678), and it carries the implication of insight that leads to righteous behavior. This wisdom is transformative, leading not only to intellectual understanding but also to character formation.

Theological Implication:

As Christ followers, we are called to embody wisdom in our lives. Wisdom is not simply knowledge but a moral and spiritual alignment with God's purposes. When we live by God's wisdom, we participate in His order, bringing peace, justice, and mercy into our relationships and communities.

6. Conclusion: Wisdom as the Bridge Between God and Humanity

In Proverbs 8, wisdom is more than an abstract principle; it is the bridge through which humanity can connect to God. As wisdom was present at creation, it continues to be available to us as a way of understanding God's will and purpose for our lives. Through Christ, who is the ultimate embodiment of wisdom, we are invited to share in God's wisdom.

Verse Reference:

"For in him all things were created: things in heaven and on earth, visible and invisible, whether thrones or powers or rulers or authorities; all things have been created through him and for him." — Colossians 1:16

Expository Insight:

Paul's description of Christ in Colossians underscores His role in creation and His preeminence. The phrase "in him all things were created" indicates that Christ, embodying divine wisdom, is both the source and the purpose of creation. This gives a fuller understanding of wisdom as being Christ-centered.

Theological Implication:

To seek wisdom is to seek Christ, the true wisdom of God. Wisdom becomes a path of discipleship, guiding us toward godly living, understanding, and reverence. As we pursue wisdom, we grow closer to God, becoming more like Christ and living out His purposes in our world.

In summary, wisdom in Proverbs 8 is portrayed as a divine attribute that, while personified, reflects God's eternal nature. Through wisdom, God ordered the world, and through Christ, the embodiment of wisdom, He redeems it. Our pursuit of wisdom is thus a pursuit of God Himself, aligning our lives with His eternal order, purpose, and beauty.

The Three Types of Wisdom in the Bible

Key Verse

"For the wisdom of this world is foolishness with God. For it is written, He taketh the wise in their own craftiness." — 1 Corinthians 3:19

The Bible presents wisdom as a multifaceted concept, not limited to a single kind or source. In exploring wisdom, we encounter three primary types: human wisdom, demonic wisdom, and godly wisdom. Each type of wisdom affects our understanding, actions, and spiritual life in different ways. This chapter aims to examine these types of wisdom from a biblical perspective, exploring how they manifest and their implications for believers.

1. Human Wisdom

Human wisdom is the understanding that people acquire through experience, observation, and reasoning. It encompasses general knowledge, common sense, and intellectual pursuits, yet is limited by human perspective and fallibility.

Verse Reference:

"What has been will be again, what has been done will be done again; there is nothing new under the sun." — Ecclesiastes 1:9

Expository Insight:

The phrase "nothing new under the sun" reflects human wisdom's limitations. While human understanding can offer practical insights, it is bound by the natural world and finite reasoning. The Hebrew word for "wisdom" here is chokmah (חָכְמָה, Strong's H2451), generally denoting skill or shrewdness. Solomon, known for his wisdom, recognizes that human insights are ultimately repetitive and transient when compared to God's eternal wisdom.

Theological Implication:

Human wisdom, while valuable for navigating everyday life, lacks the capacity to grasp eternal truths fully. As Solomon points out in Ecclesiastes 3:19-20, human wisdom alone leads us to recognize that we are limited and mortal. For instance, "For what happens to the children of man and what happens to the beasts is the same… All go to one place; all are from the dust, and to dust all return." This acknowledgment of limitation should drive believers to seek wisdom beyond human understanding.

2. Demonic Wisdom

Demonic wisdom is described as the wisdom of this world that opposes God's truth. It is deceitful, often seeking to corrupt, manipulate, or control. Demonic wisdom stems from spiritual forces of evil, aligning with worldly values and selfish ambitions.

Verse Reference:

"This wisdom does not descend from above, but is earthly, sensual, demonic." — James 3:15

Expository Insight:

James contrasts "earthly, sensual, demonic" wisdom with godly wisdom, which is "pure, peaceable, gentle, willing to yield, full of mercy and good fruits, without partiality and hypocrisy" (James 3:17). The Greek term used here for "demonic" (daimoniōdēs, δαιμονιώδης, Strong's G1141) signifies something influenced or driven by demonic forces. This type of wisdom is self-centered, divisive, and driven by pride or envy.

Theological Implication:

The Bible warns believers about demonic wisdom, which leads people away from God's truth and into spiritual darkness. Paul references this in 1 Corinthians 2:6, explaining, "We speak wisdom among those who are mature, yet not the wisdom of this age, nor of the rulers of this age, who are coming to nothing." Ephesians 6:12 reminds us that "we wrestle not against flesh and blood, but against principalities, against powers, against the rulers of the darkness of this world." Believers must guard against this false wisdom by discerning what aligns with God's Spirit and what does not.

3. Godly Wisdom

Godly wisdom, or divine wisdom, originates from God and is given to those who seek it with a sincere heart. This wisdom leads to spiritual discernment, aligning our thoughts, actions, and attitudes with God's truth and purpose.

Verse Reference:

"The wisdom that is from above is first pure, then peaceable, gentle, willing to yield, full of mercy and good fruits, without partiality and without hypocrisy." — James 3:17

Expository Insight:

The Greek word for "wisdom" here is sophia (σοφία, Strong's G4678), which implies insight into divine truths. James lists qualities associated with godly wisdom: purity, peace, gentleness, and sincerity. Godly wisdom is transformative, shaping our character to reflect Christ's nature and empowering us to live according to God's standards.

Theological Implication:

Godly wisdom is the type of wisdom believers should pursue. Paul explains in 1 Corinthians 2:14 that "the natural man does not receive the things of the Spirit of God, for they are foolishness to him." Divine wisdom is spiritually discerned and requires a heart attuned to God. This wisdom not only informs our understanding but leads us to a life that glorifies God. Proverbs 9:10 reinforces this: "The fear of the

Lord is the beginning of wisdom." Reverence for God opens the door to understanding His ways and purposes.

4. Comparing the Three Types of Wisdom

Each type of wisdom has distinct characteristics and produces different outcomes. Human wisdom can provide insights for daily life but lacks the depth needed for spiritual growth. Demonic wisdom seeks to deceive and corrupt, drawing individuals away from God. Godly wisdom, however, leads to truth, peace, and a deeper relationship with God.

Type	Source	Characteristics	Outcome
Human Wisdom	Human experience	Practical, limited, transient	Temporary solutions, limited insight
Demonic Wisdom	Evil spiritual forces	Deceptive, divisive, self-centered	Spiritual darkness, moral corruption
Godly Wisdom	God's Spirit	Pure, peaceable, gentle, merciful	Spiritual growth, alignment with God's will

Practical Application:

Believers must discern which type of wisdom they are following. Human wisdom, while beneficial, must not replace godly wisdom. Demonic wisdom should be rejected, as it leads away from God's truth. Godly wisdom should be sought through prayer, study, and reverence for God, as it aligns our lives with His eternal purposes.

5. Pursuing Godly Wisdom in Daily Life

Proverbs 4:7 urges us, "Wisdom is the principal thing; therefore get wisdom: and with all thy getting get understanding." True wisdom involves seeking God's perspective, which transcends human reasoning and exposes the lies of demonic wisdom.

Verse Reference:

"If any of you lacks wisdom, let him ask of God, who gives to all liberally and without reproach, and it will be given to him." — James 1:5

Expository Insight:

James encourages believers to seek wisdom directly from God, who generously grants it. The Greek word for "lacks" here, leipetai (λείπεται, Strong's G3007), implies a shortfall or deficiency. Recognizing our need for God's wisdom is the first step toward receiving it, as God is faithful to provide insight and understanding to those who ask sincerely.

Theological Implication:

Godly wisdom is accessible to all who humbly seek it. Unlike human or demonic wisdom, godly wisdom requires a surrender of self-will and a commitment to follow God's ways. Through prayer, scripture, and the guidance of the Holy Spirit, believers can cultivate godly wisdom, which enables them to live in alignment with God's truth.

6. Conclusion: Embracing Godly Wisdom

The Bible teaches that wisdom is not merely an intellectual pursuit but a matter of the heart and spirit. Each type of wisdom—human, demonic, and godly—has its source, characteristics, and impact on our lives. By pursuing godly wisdom, believers find not only knowledge but transformation, drawing closer to God and living in harmony with His purposes.

Final Reflection:

"The fear of the Lord is the beginning of wisdom, and the knowledge of the Holy One is understanding." —

Proverbs 9:10 ...of the Holy Spirit, believers can grow in godly wisdom, which brings true insight and lasting peace.

6. The Role of the Holy Spirit in Imparting Wisdom

The Holy Spirit is the source and guide of godly wisdom, helping believers understand spiritual truths and apply them in everyday life. Jesus promised that the Holy Spirit would "teach you all things" (John 14:26), equipping us to discern between true wisdom and false wisdom.

Verse Reference:

"But the Helper, the Holy Spirit, whom the Father will send in My name, He will teach you all things, and bring to your remembrance all things that I said to you." — John 14:26

Expository Insight:

The Greek word for "Helper" (Paraklētos, παράκλητος, Strong's G3875) signifies an advocate, teacher, or one who comes alongside. The Holy Spirit provides insight that human wisdom cannot grasp, illuminating God's Word and revealing truths that lead to spiritual maturity.

Theological Implication:

The Holy Spirit enables believers to receive divine wisdom by guiding us into all truth (John 16:13). This wisdom isn't just theoretical; it transforms our lives, helping us to walk in obedience and bring glory to God. As Paul explains in 1 Corinthians 2:10-11, "God has revealed them to us through His Spirit. For the Spirit searches all things, yes, the deep things of God."

7. The Fruit of Godly Wisdom

Godly wisdom produces the fruit of the Spirit, fostering peace, patience, kindness, and other attributes aligned with God's character. James 3:17 describes godly wisdom as pure, peaceable, gentle, and full of mercy, reflecting a life transformed by God.

Verse Reference:

"But the wisdom that is from above is first pure, then peaceable, gentle, willing to yield, full of mercy and good fruits, without partiality and without hypocrisy." — James 3:17

Expository Insight:

Each characteristic of godly wisdom has a direct impact on relationships and community. The word "pure" (hagnos, ἁγνός, Strong's G53) implies holiness or moral integrity, while "peaceable" (eirēnikos, εἰρηνικός, Strong's G1516) refers to the pursuit of peace. Together, these qualities represent a life governed by divine wisdom, contributing to harmony and building up others in love.

Theological Implication:

The fruit of godly wisdom serves as a witness to others, demonstrating the impact of God's truth in our lives. When believers operate with this wisdom, they reflect God's character to the world, glorifying Him and drawing others to the faith.

8. Practical Steps to Seek Godly Wisdom

1. Prayer and Dependence on God: Ask God for wisdom as James 1:5 instructs, recognizing that it is a gift from Him. Trust in God's generosity to provide guidance in all situations.

2. Study Scripture Diligently: The Bible is the ultimate source of godly wisdom. By meditating on God's Word, we align our thoughts with His eternal truths.

3. Submit to the Holy Spirit: Allow the Holy Spirit to guide your decisions and thoughts, seeking His leading in all areas of life.

4. Embrace Humility: Recognize our limitations and depend on God's wisdom rather than our own. Humility opens the door for God to reveal His insights.

The three types of wisdom in the Bible—human, demonic, and godly—present us with choices that shape our lives and our relationship with God. Human wisdom, though useful, is limited in its reach. Demonic wisdom deceives and leads away from God, creating confusion and strife. Godly wisdom, however, is a gift from God that aligns us with His purpose, enriches our spiritual lives, and brings peace.

As we pursue godly wisdom, we grow in understanding and discernment, reflecting God's character in a world that often values other forms of wisdom. By revering God and seeking His wisdom above all else, we can live a life that is not only wise by human standards but also deeply rooted in spiritual truth. As Proverbs 4:7 reminds us, "Wisdom is the principal thing; therefore get wisdom: and with all thy getting get understanding." This wisdom from God leads us to a life of purpose, peace, and eternal significance.

CHAPTER 06

THE BENEFITS OF WISDOM

"Blessed are those who listen to me, watching daily at my doors, waiting at my doorway. For those who find me find life and receive favor from the Lord."

— Proverbs 8:34-35

The pursuit of wisdom is far from an abstract or philosophical exercise. According to Proverbs, those who seek and apply wisdom experience tangible, real-world benefits in every area of their lives. Wisdom is described as a faithful guide, offering blessing, protection, and guidance to those who seek it with patience and humility. Proverbs 8:34-

35 highlights how living a wise life leads to blessings, favor, and abundant life.

In this chapter, we'll explore the benefits that wisdom offers, ranging from personal peace and well-being to divine favor and strengthened relationships. By grounding our understanding of wisdom in scripture, we'll see how the blessings it brings are both practical and spiritual, impacting daily decisions and deepening our relationship with God.

1. Wisdom Brings Divine Favor

The Bible consistently associates wisdom with favor from God. Those who walk in wisdom are often described as blessed or favored, experiencing God's provision and support in their lives.

Verse Reference:

"Blessed are those who listen to me, watching daily at my doors, waiting at my doorway. For those who find me find life and receive favor from the Lord." — Proverbs 8:34-35

Expository Insight:

In Hebrew, the word for "blessed" here is 'esher (אֶשֶׁר, Strong's H835), which conveys a sense of happiness, fulfillment, and divine blessing. Wisdom, therefore, is not just about intellect or cleverness; it is a path that leads to a fulfilled life marked by God's approval and favor. Those who "listen" and "wait" upon wisdom are portrayed as actively seeking guidance, trusting in wisdom to direct their steps.

Theological Insight:

In both the Old and New Testaments, the concept of divine favor is closely tied to obedience and humility. Just as wisdom calls us to live in harmony with God's principles, favor is the result of aligning our lives with His will. The blessings of wisdom are not rewards for mere knowledge but the outcome of living in alignment with God's truth.

2. Wisdom Provides Protection

A life guided by wisdom is often a life protected from harm, as wise choices can steer us away from dangerous situations and poor decisions.

Verse Reference:

"Discretion will protect you, and understanding will guard you." — Proverbs 2:11

Expository Insight:

The term "discretion" (mezimmah, מְזִמָּה, Strong's H4209) refers to prudence or sound judgment, qualities that help a person anticipate consequences and avoid unnecessary risks. This protection is not a physical shield but a form of guidance that steers individuals away from harm and leads them along paths of safety.

Theological Insight:

The Bible often emphasizes that God's laws and wisdom act as safeguards for His people. By living within the boundaries of wisdom, believers avoid the pitfalls of sin and poor choices. Wisdom is, in this sense, a form of divine guidance and protection, keeping those who seek it from straying into harm's way.

3. Wisdom Leads to Life and Peace

True wisdom enriches life and brings inner peace, allowing individuals to experience contentment regardless of their circumstances. Unlike material wealth, wisdom offers a lasting sense of fulfillment that transcends external conditions.

Verse Reference:

"Long life is in her right hand; in her left hand are riches and honor." — Proverbs 3:16

Expository Insight:

The phrase "long life" (orek yamim, יָמִים אֹרֶךְ, Strong's H753) implies not just physical longevity but a life marked by richness, purpose, and fulfillment. "Riches" and "honor" are also symbols of well-being and respect, suggesting that wisdom brings rewards beyond material wealth or social status.

Theological Insight:

God's wisdom creates harmony within our souls, leading to peace. The New Testament echoes this sentiment when Paul describes the "peace of God, which surpasses all understanding" (Philippians 4:7). Wisdom grants an inner tranquility that material success cannot replicate, rooted in a life that is well-aligned with God's purpose.

4. Wisdom Promotes Strong Relationships

Wisdom cultivates virtues like patience, kindness, and empathy, which foster healthier relationships and build community. A wise person is often slow to anger, quick to listen, and careful in speech, qualities that nurture harmony and trust.

Verse Reference:

"A gentle answer turns away wrath, but a harsh word stirs up anger." — Proverbs 15:1

Expository Insight:

The Hebrew word for "gentle" here, rak (רַךְ, Strong's H7390), refers to something soft or tender. Wisdom often manifests in gentle, considerate responses that de-escalate conflicts and promote understanding. Conversely, "harsh" (etsev, עֶצֶב, Strong's H6089) implies pain or hardship, suggesting that a lack of wisdom can cause relational tension.

Theological Insight:

Jesus exemplified wisdom in His relationships, showing compassion, patience, and love. By following His example, believers are empowered to build strong relationships that reflect God's love. The book of James also emphasizes that "the wisdom from above is first pure, then peaceable, gentle, open to reason" (James 3:17), underscoring that wise interactions are essential for godly relationships.

5. Wisdom Brings Spiritual Insight

Wisdom allows us to see life from God's perspective, understanding His will and purposes more clearly. This spiritual insight enhances our faith, helping us to trust God more deeply and walk in obedience to His commandments.

Verse Reference:

"Trust in the Lord with all your heart and lean not on your own understanding; in all your ways submit to him, and he will make your paths straight." — Proverbs 3:5-6

Expository Insight:

The phrase "lean not on your own understanding" suggests a reliance on divine guidance rather than human logic. Wisdom goes beyond human reason, guiding believers to rely on God's knowledge, which is perfect and comprehensive.

Theological Insight:

Wisdom brings clarity to God's will, helping believers discern spiritual truths and align themselves with His eternal plan. Spiritual insight is not about knowing every detail of the future but about trusting that God's wisdom is sufficient for each step of the journey.

Practical Steps to Cultivate Wisdom and Its Benefits

1. Daily Seek God's Guidance: Like those who "wait at the doorway" (Proverbs 8:34), set aside time each day to seek God's wisdom in prayer, asking Him to guide your thoughts and decisions.

2. Study God's Word: The Bible is a primary source of wisdom. By reading and meditating on scripture, we gain insights that shape our lives and lead to wise living.

3. Practice Humility: Humility opens the door to receiving wisdom, as pride often blinds us to our need for God's guidance.

4. Surround Yourself with Wise Counsel: Seek advice from those who are mature in faith, as Proverbs 13:20 encourages, "Walk with the wise and become wise."

5. Reflect and Apply: Make a habit of reflecting on how God's wisdom has guided you in the past, reinforcing the benefits of wise living in your present decisions.

The benefits of wisdom are profound and wide-ranging, impacting every aspect of life—from personal peace and divine favor to stronger relationships and spiritual insight. In Proverbs 8, wisdom offers life, favor, and protection, blessing those who pursue it with a life marked by purpose, peace, and alignment with God's will. By embracing the pursuit of wisdom, we align ourselves with God's design for a fulfilling, godly life.

The blessings of wisdom go beyond knowledge or intellect; they bring us into a life that reflects God's character and leads us into His favor. As we seek wisdom, we're reminded of Jesus' promise that "I came that they may have life and have it abundantly" (John 10:10). Wisdom, therefore, is not just beneficial—it is essential to a life of faith and fellowship with God.

The Benefits of Wisdom

"Blessed are those who listen to me, watching daily at my doors, waiting at my doorway. For those who find me find life and receive favor from the Lord."

— Proverbs 8:34-35

The pursuit of wisdom brings a wealth of benefits that extend to nearly every aspect of our lives. Wisdom is not just a theoretical concept but a practical guide that shapes how we approach life's challenges, relationships, and personal growth.

As Proverbs repeatedly emphasizes, wisdom is a source of life, favor, and well-being for those who seek it.

In this chapter, we will explore the diverse ways in which wisdom blesses those who pursue it. From making sound decisions to cultivating inner peace and joy, wisdom serves as a transformative force that aligns us more closely with God's purpose for our lives.

1. Making Better Decisions

One of the primary benefits of wisdom is the ability to make decisions that are good for both the present and the future. Through discernment, wisdom provides clarity and direction, helping us to make choices that align with God's will.

Verse Reference:

"Trust in the Lord with all your heart and lean not on your own understanding; in all your ways submit to him, and he will make your paths straight." — Proverbs 3:5-6

Expository Insight:

The Hebrew term for "understanding" (biynah, בִּינָה, Strong's H998) refers to discernment or insight. By trusting in God and seeking His wisdom, we gain a deeper understanding that goes beyond our limited perspective. This results in a more stable and purposeful path, as God directs our steps.

Application:

Wisdom equips us to avoid impulsive choices and instead consider the potential long-term impacts of our decisions. In doing so, it protects us from unnecessary hardships and guides us in ways that honor God and benefit others.

2. Contributing to Your Community

Wisdom enables us to live selflessly, balancing our needs with those of others. This fosters a sense of community, as wisdom prompts us to act with kindness, fairness, and understanding toward those around us.

Verse Reference:

"Each of you should look not only to your own interests, but also to the interests of others." — Philippians 2:4

Expository Insight:

The Greek word for "interests" (skopos, σκοπός, Strong's G4649) implies focusing on or paying close attention to others' needs. Wisdom encourages us to cultivate empathy, strengthening our communities through service and mutual respect.

Application:

When we apply wisdom in our relationships and responsibilities, we contribute positively to the well-being of our families, workplaces, and communities. Wisdom inspires us to seek harmony and serve others, reflecting God's love in our actions.

3. Recovering from Failure

Wisdom empowers us to learn from mistakes and approach setbacks with resilience. Rather than becoming discouraged, a wise person can see failure as an opportunity for growth, using past experiences as a foundation for future success.

Verse Reference:

"For though the righteous fall seven times, they rise again, but the wicked stumble when calamity strikes." — Proverbs 24:16

Expository Insight:

The term "rise" (quwm, קוּם, Strong's H6965) signifies strength and restoration. Wisdom allows the righteous to bounce back from failure by relying on God's grace and guidance. Rather than being paralyzed by mistakes, wisdom enables us to reflect, adapt, and improve.

Application:

Wisdom encourages a mindset that values growth and persistence. It fosters resilience by teaching us to view failure as a stepping stone, not a roadblock, thus building endurance and strengthening our character.

4. Cultivating Joy and Trust

True wisdom leads to a life marked by joy, contentment, and trust in God. By understanding and embracing God's purposes, we find lasting peace and a sense of fulfillment that transcends circumstances.

Verse Reference:

"Joyful is the person who finds wisdom, the one who gains understanding." — Proverbs 3:13

Expository Insight:

The Hebrew word for "joyful" (ashre, אַשְׁרֵי, Strong's H835) connotes a sense of happiness and blessedness. Wisdom brings joy by aligning us with God's will, which is the source of true peace and contentment.

Application:

Wisdom helps us cultivate an attitude of gratitude and trust, even in difficult situations. By focusing on God's goodness and promises, we experience inner joy and a calm assurance that God is in control.

5. Understanding Others

Wisdom enhances our ability to understand the emotions, motives, and needs of others. By fostering empathy, it helps us make thoughtful social decisions and build meaningful relationships.

Verse Reference:

"A person's wisdom yields patience; it is to one's glory to overlook an offense." — Proverbs 19:11

Expository Insight:

The word "patience" here is derived from arak (אָרֵךְ, Strong's H750), meaning to be long-suffering or slow to anger. Wisdom enables us to approach others with patience and understanding, recognizing their humanity and extending grace.

Application:

By deepening our empathy, wisdom helps us navigate complex social situations with kindness and respect. This not only strengthens our relationships but also enables us to respond to others with a heart that mirrors God's love and compassion.

6. Developing Self-Control

Wisdom empowers us to exercise self-control, helping us resist impulsive behavior and manage our reactions, especially in challenging situations.

Verse Reference:

"Like a city whose walls are broken through is a person who lacks self-control." — Proverbs 25:28

Expository Insight:

The metaphor of a "city without walls" represents vulnerability and chaos. Self-control, as imparted by wisdom, acts as a protective barrier, enabling us to govern our thoughts and actions instead of being ruled by them.

Application:

Wisdom instills discipline, allowing us to pause and consider the consequences of our actions. This helps us maintain integrity, exercise patience, and make choices that align with our values and faith.

7. Fostering Self-Knowledge

Wisdom encourages introspection, helping us gain insight into our own hearts, strengths, weaknesses, and motivations. Through self-reflection, we grow in our understanding of who we are in relation to God.

Verse Reference:

"Examine yourselves to see whether you are in the faith; test yourselves." — 2 Corinthians 13:5

Expository Insight:

The Greek term for "examine" (peirazo, πειράζω, Strong's G3985) implies a careful scrutiny or testing. Wisdom promotes self-awareness, guiding us to evaluate our intentions and actions to ensure they are consistent with our faith.

Application:

Wisdom aids us in self-reflection, which is essential for spiritual growth and integrity. By understanding ourselves better, we can make positive changes, avoid self-deception, and strengthen our relationship with God.

The benefits of wisdom encompass every aspect of life, from personal growth to improved relationships and resilience in the face of challenges. A life guided by wisdom is one marked by purpose, joy, and divine favor, as we align ourselves more closely with God's will.

The pursuit of wisdom is a lifelong journey that brings blessings both tangible and spiritual. By embracing wisdom, we open ourselves to God's guidance, protection, and love, experiencing the fullness of life He intends for us. Through wisdom, we not only enrich our own lives but also positively impact the lives of those around us, bringing light and hope to our communities.

Wisdom Helps You Work Smarter, Not Harder

"If the iron is blunt, and one does not sharpen the edge, he must use more strength, but wisdom helps one to succeed." — Ecclesiastes 10:10

One of the most practical benefits of wisdom is its ability to guide us toward efficient and effective action. Wisdom is not merely knowledge but the skillful application of understanding to accomplish meaningful goals without unnecessary exertion. As Ecclesiastes 10:10 illustrates, a sharpened edge—symbolizing wisdom—enables a person to work smarter rather than harder. In this chapter, we'll delve into the role of wisdom in guiding us to work efficiently, make calculated decisions, and achieve results with purpose.

1. Wisdom Sharpens Our Efforts

The metaphor of a blunt iron in Ecclesiastes 10:10 speaks to the need for preparation, strategy, and reflection. Working without wisdom is like trying to cut with a dull blade: it requires more effort and is ultimately less effective.

Verse Reference:

"If the iron is blunt, and one does not sharpen the edge, he must use more strength, but wisdom helps one to succeed." — Ecclesiastes 10:10

Expository Insight:

The word "sharpens" (Hebrew: qashah, קָשָׁה, Strong's H7185) implies making something effective or precise. The verse underscores that wisdom is like sharpening a tool, making our efforts more productive. By sharpening our minds and hearts with wisdom, we gain clarity, making our work more focused and impactful.

Application:

Wisdom encourages us to invest time in preparation, planning, and learning before taking action. Instead of exerting energy on trial and error, wisdom helps us approach tasks thoughtfully, minimizing wasted effort.

2. Strategic Thinking and Planning

Wisdom equips us to assess situations and plan accordingly, guiding us to make decisions that maximize efficiency and minimize setbacks. This strategic approach is aligned with God's design, where thoughtful planning precedes successful endeavors.

Verse Reference:

"The plans of the diligent lead to profit as surely as haste leads to poverty." — Proverbs 21:5

Expository Insight:

The Hebrew word for "diligent" (charuts, חָרוּץ, Strong's H2742) refers to someone who is prudent and hardworking. Wisdom teaches us to balance diligence with careful planning, leading to "profit," or productive outcomes, rather than haste, which often results in failure or wasted resources.

Application:

When we approach tasks and goals with wisdom, we're more likely to achieve long-lasting success. Wisdom teaches us to consider all angles, weigh the pros and cons, and proceed with caution, helping us avoid mistakes and reduce unnecessary hardship.

3. Efficiency in Action

Working smarter means recognizing that efficiency is not about rushing but about aligning actions with a clear purpose and using the best methods. Wisdom empowers us to make the most of our time and energy, finding effective solutions to complex problems.

Verse Reference:

"Walk in wisdom toward outsiders, making the best use of the time." — Colossians 4:5

Expository Insight:

The Greek word for "time" (kairos, καιρός, Strong's G2540) refers to an opportune moment. Wisdom encourages us to recognize opportunities and to act efficiently in seizing them. It's about prioritizing actions that serve God's purpose and using resources effectively.

Application:

Efficiency through wisdom helps us eliminate distractions and focus on what truly matters. By identifying key priorities and using time wisely, we increase productivity and maintain a balanced, God-centered life.

4. Prudence in Decisions

Wisdom fosters prudence, teaching us to avoid hasty decisions and instead deliberate thoughtfully. Prudence is often associated with practical wisdom, which helps us make sound choices in day-to-day matters.

Verse Reference:

"The prudent see danger and take refuge, but the simple keep going and pay the penalty." — Proverbs 22:3

Expository Insight:

The Hebrew term for "prudent" (arum, עָרוּם, Strong's H6175) means one who is shrewd or sensible. Wisdom enhances our ability to anticipate consequences and avoid reckless actions. The prudent individual is proactive, foreseeing potential dangers and preparing accordingly.

Application:

Wisdom calls us to carefully evaluate options, foresee potential challenges, and make informed choices. This prevents us from unnecessary setbacks, allowing us to avoid difficulties that could have been anticipated and mitigated.

5. Seeking Guidance and Counsel

One of the most important aspects of working smarter is recognizing when to seek guidance. Wisdom teaches us to value the counsel of others, acknowledging that collaboration often leads to better solutions.

Verse Reference:

"Plans fail for lack of counsel, but with many advisers they succeed." — Proverbs 15:22

Expository Insight:

The word for "counsel" (etsah, עֵצָה, Strong's H6098) signifies advice or guidance. Wisdom doesn't operate in isolation; it seeks diverse perspectives and experiences, drawing on collective insight to achieve success.

Application:

Wisdom encourages us to be open to advice, seeing value in the insights of others. By doing so, we expand our understanding, avoid potential pitfalls, and strengthen our decisions through the wisdom shared by those we trust.

6. Self-Control and Focus

Working smarter requires focus and self-discipline, allowing us to resist distractions and commit ourselves fully to our tasks. Wisdom fosters self-control, guiding us to remain dedicated to our goals.

Verse Reference:

"Like a city whose walls are broken through is a person who lacks self-control." — Proverbs 25:28

Expository Insight:

The imagery of a "city with broken walls" symbolizes vulnerability and lack of order. Wisdom instills self-control, which serves as a safeguard, allowing us to channel our energy toward constructive activities and resist impulsive distractions.

Application:

By cultivating self-discipline, wisdom enables us to stay focused on our goals, helping us work more effectively and efficiently. This not only leads to productivity but also fosters spiritual growth as we prioritize God's purposes over fleeting distractions.

7. Overcoming Obstacles with Insight

Wisdom provides insight that helps us navigate obstacles and challenges with discernment, finding creative solutions rather than becoming overwhelmed. This resilience is a hallmark of working smarter, as we learn to adapt and persevere.

Verse Reference:

"If any of you lacks wisdom, let him ask God, who gives generously to all without reproach, and it will be given him." — James 1:5

Expository Insight:

The Greek word for "wisdom" here (sophia, σοφία, Strong's G4678) encompasses knowledge, skill, and practical application. God's wisdom equips us to overcome challenges with insight, strengthening us to persevere and succeed even when circumstances are difficult.

Application:

Wisdom encourages us to approach challenges with creativity and resilience, asking God for guidance and relying on His strength. By trusting in His wisdom, we find that obstacles become opportunities for growth and achievement.

8. Recognizing God's Role in Success

Ultimately, working smarter means acknowledging that our success comes from God's wisdom and blessing. It involves aligning our efforts with His will and relying on His guidance for true success.

Verse Reference:

"Commit to the Lord whatever you do, and he will establish your plans." — Proverbs 16:3

Expository Insight:

The Hebrew term for "commit" (galal, גָּלַל, Strong's H1556) implies rolling one's work onto the Lord, surrendering it to Him. Wisdom teaches us to depend on God, recognizing that our success is established not solely by our efforts but by His grace.

Application:

Working smarter ultimately involves seeking God's blessing and direction in all we do. By committing our plans to Him, we ensure that our work is not only efficient but also aligned with His eternal purposes.

Wisdom transforms how we approach our work and life by enabling us to work smarter rather than harder. Through wisdom, we learn to be efficient, strategic, and prudent, prioritizing what matters and relying on God for guidance and success. Wisdom invites us to sharpen our spiritual and practical skills, leading to a life marked by effectiveness, fulfillment, and divine purpose.

By embracing wisdom, we find that our efforts yield greater results with less strain, allowing us to live in harmony with God's will and experience the fullness of His blessings.

CHAPTER 07

WISDOM AND RIGHTEOUSNESS

"Counsel and sound judgment are mine; I have insight, I have power. By me kings reign and rulers issue decrees that are just."

— Proverbs 8:14-15

Wisdom is inseparably connected to righteousness and justice, forming the foundation of ethical leadership and decision-making. When leaders embrace wisdom, they are empowered not only to make sound decisions but also to bring justice and peace to those they lead. Proverbs 8:14-15 shows that wisdom provides "counsel," "sound judgment," and "insight," all of which contribute to true power. This chapter explores how wisdom fosters righteous leadership, drawing from biblical and historical examples, and offers insights for contemporary leaders in every field.

1. The Source of Righteous Leadership

In Proverbs 8:14, wisdom declares that counsel, sound judgment, insight, and power are its attributes. Here, wisdom speaks as an agent of God, highlighting that true leadership qualities—judgment, power, and insight—are not merely human skills but gifts from God.

Verse Reference:

"Counsel and sound judgment are mine; I have insight, I have power." — Proverbs 8:14

Expository Insight:

The term "counsel" (Hebrew: etsah, עֵצָה, Strong's H6098) indicates purpose or guidance, and "sound judgment" (Hebrew: tushiyah, תּוּשִׁיָּה, Strong's H8454) represents wisdom that brings stability. This highlights the balanced nature of wisdom—it guides leaders not just to make effective decisions but to do so with stability and foresight.

Application:

Leaders who recognize that wisdom comes from God seek guidance from Him, valuing His input above human understanding. This spiritual foundation is crucial, as it sets the stage for righteous decision-making that reflects God's character.

2. Wisdom in Establishing Justice

Biblical wisdom consistently emphasizes justice as a core value of righteous leadership. Kings, judges, and prophets were often charged with upholding justice, and those who sought wisdom were able to do so effectively.

Verse Reference:

"By me kings reign and rulers issue decrees that are just." — Proverbs 8:15

Expository Insight:

The word "reign" (Hebrew: malak, מָלַךְ, Strong's H4427) implies governing or having dominion. In a godly sense, reigning involves upholding justice, ensuring that power is exercised fairly and equitably. Wisdom grants rulers the discernment needed to create and enforce laws that protect the welfare of their people.

Application:

In all forms of leadership, wisdom acts as a compass for fairness. Wise leaders consider the impact of their decisions on others, striving to establish policies and practices that are just and impartial.

3. Examples of Righteous Leadership in the Bible

The Bible provides numerous examples of leaders who embodied wisdom and righteousness, including King Solomon and King David. Their reigns were characterized by decisions that brought justice and peace to their people.

King Solomon's Request for Wisdom

When Solomon became king, he prayed for wisdom to govern his people justly, prioritizing their well-being over personal gain.

Verse Reference:

"So give your servant a discerning heart to govern your people and to distinguish between right and wrong." — 1 Kings 3:9

Expository Insight:

The phrase "discerning heart" (Hebrew: leb shomea, שֹׁמֵעַ לֵב, Strong's H3820 and H8085) refers to a heart that listens and understands. Solomon's prayer demonstrated humility and a desire to lead with godly wisdom, not through power alone.

Application:

Solomon's example encourages leaders to seek discernment in decision-making, placing the needs of those they serve above their own ambitions.

Moses as a Leader of Justice

Moses was a shepherd-leader who, with God's guidance, implemented laws that promoted justice and protected the rights of individuals.

Verse Reference:

"Moses chose able men from all Israel and made them heads over the people… They judged the people at all times." — Exodus 18:25-26

Expository Insight:

The Hebrew word for "judge" (shaphat, שָׁפַט, Strong's H8199) means to govern or render justice. Moses' system of delegation, based on wisdom, ensured that justice was accessible to all, preventing unfair burdens on both the people and the leaders.

Application:

Moses' wisdom in establishing a structured system for judgment and fairness is a model for leaders in creating frameworks that distribute responsibility and uphold equity.

4. The Role of Wisdom in Creating Peace

Wise leadership does not merely enforce laws; it fosters peace by promoting unity and compassion. Wisdom leads to decisions that harmonize diverse needs, fostering environments of mutual respect and trust.

Verse Reference:

"Peacemakers who sow in peace reap a harvest of righteousness." — James 3:18

Expository Insight:

The Greek word for "peace" (eirene, εἰρήνη, Strong's G1515) signifies harmony and absence of conflict. Wisdom aligns with righteousness in promoting peace, creating a context where communities can thrive without division or strife.

Application:

Wise leaders seek peaceful resolutions rather than exacerbating conflict. By embodying compassion and understanding, they establish trust and strengthen their communities.

5. Resisting Corruption through Wisdom

Wisdom serves as a safeguard against the misuse of power, emphasizing integrity and accountability in leadership. Leaders grounded in wisdom are less likely to fall into corruption or manipulation.

Verse Reference:

"Do not pervert justice or show partiality… Follow justice and justice alone." — Deuteronomy 16:19-20

Expository Insight:

The Hebrew word for "justice" (mishpat, מִשְׁפָּט, Strong's H4941) refers to moral righteousness and fairness. Leaders who embrace wisdom maintain a commitment to uprightness, resisting the temptation to compromise on ethical principles.

Application:

Wisdom equips leaders to uphold integrity, rejecting favoritism and corruption. Wise leaders cultivate accountability, ensuring that their actions remain aligned with godly standards.

6. Wisdom as a Model for Modern Leadership

The principles of wisdom found in Scripture are timeless and apply to all forms of leadership today, whether in government, business, education, or family. Leaders who embrace godly wisdom find themselves capable of making decisions that benefit those they serve.

Verse Reference:

"Let the wise listen and add to their learning, and let the discerning get guidance." — Proverbs 1:5

Expository Insight:

The term "learning" (Hebrew: leqach, לֶקַח, Strong's H3948) denotes knowledge gained through instruction or experience. Wisdom is not static; it requires continual growth and openness to new understanding.

Application:

Modern leaders who practice wisdom are teachable, continually seeking knowledge to adapt to new challenges. This flexibility allows them to lead effectively, balancing tradition with innovation.

7. The Connection Between Wisdom and the Fear of the Lord

At the heart of righteous leadership is reverence for God, acknowledging that true wisdom originates from Him. Leaders grounded in the fear of the Lord lead with humility, understanding that their authority is ultimately accountable to a higher power.

Verse Reference:

"The fear of the Lord is the beginning of wisdom, and knowledge of the Holy One is understanding." — Proverbs 9:10

Expository Insight:

The Hebrew word for "fear" (yirah, יִרְאָה, Strong's H3374) implies reverence and awe. When leaders approach their roles with a deep respect for God's authority, they make decisions that align with His righteousness and purpose.

Application:

The fear of the Lord fosters a spirit of humility and accountability, reminding leaders that their position is a trust from God. This mindset nurtures decisions that are righteous, just, and compassionate.

Righteous leadership is not merely about wielding authority but about guiding others in a way that reflects God's justice, compassion, and integrity. Proverbs 8:14-15 captures the essence of wise leadership, where counsel, sound judgment, and justice are gifts from God bestowed on those who seek Him. By embracing wisdom, leaders—whether kings, parents, teachers, or business owners—can bring peace, justice, and equity to their spheres of influence. As seen through biblical and historical examples, wisdom equips leaders to make decisions that honor God and uplift others, building a legacy of righteousness that endures.

By aspiring to the wisdom described in Proverbs, today's leaders can reflect God's character in every decision, fostering environments of trust, justice, and compassion.

Wisdom as a Foundation for Security and Well-Being

"My son, keep sound wisdom and discretion…Then you will walk on your way securely, and your foot will not stumble. If you lie down, you will not be afraid; when you lie down, your sleep will be sweet. Do not be afraid of sudden terror or of the ruin of the wicked, when it comes, for the Lord will be your confidence and will keep your foot from being caught."

— Proverbs 3:21-26

Wisdom in the Bible extends beyond intellectual knowledge or moral insight; it is a deeply practical guide that provides believers with stability, personal security, and a sense of well-being. Proverbs 3:21-26 emphasizes that wisdom is not only about understanding God's principles but also about living a life anchored in His truth, which brings peace even amid life's uncertainties. This chapter explores how wisdom provides security and stability in various aspects of life, using a combination of expository insights and in-depth analysis based on biblical references.

1. The Role of Wisdom and Discretion

Proverbs 3:21 urges us to "keep sound wisdom and discretion," implying that these qualities are essential safeguards in daily life. The terms "wisdom" and "discretion" here are paired to represent a balanced, thoughtful approach to decision-making and moral living.

Verse Reference:

"My son, keep sound wisdom and discretion…" — Proverbs 3:21

Expository Insight:

The Hebrew word for "wisdom" (hokmah, חׇכְמָה, Strong's H2451) refers to skillful knowledge, while "discretion" (mezimmah, מְזִמָּה, Strong's H4209) implies purposeful planning or prudence. Together, these qualities help an individual navigate life's complexities with clear thinking and moral integrity.

Application:

When believers maintain wisdom and discretion, they are less likely to make impulsive or reckless choices. Wisdom provides insight, while discretion allows for thoughtful action, ensuring that one's path is both secure and aligned with God's will.

2. Walking Securely and Avoiding Pitfalls

The promise in Proverbs 3:23 that one's "foot will not stumble" highlights the security that comes from following wisdom. This is not simply a physical assurance but an affirmation of emotional and spiritual stability.

Verse Reference:

"Then you will walk on your way securely, and your foot will not stumble." — Proverbs 3:23

Expository Insight:

The term "securely" (Hebrew: betah, בֶּטַח, Strong's H983) conveys confidence or trust. Walking securely in biblical terms signifies living with a firm sense of purpose, free from anxiety and fear. In the context of wisdom, this suggests that those who follow God's principles avoid unnecessary pitfalls.

Application:

By aligning our choices with God's wisdom, we avoid moral and emotional "stumbling." This does not guarantee a life free from challenges, but it assures us that wisdom will guide us through difficult times without fear or regret.

3. Freedom from Fear and Anxiety

One of the most profound benefits of wisdom is freedom from fear. Proverbs 3:24-25 highlights that those who live by wisdom experience restful sleep, free from anxiety or dread of sudden calamity.

Verse Reference:

"If you lie down, you will not be afraid; when you lie down, your sleep will be sweet." — Proverbs 3:24

Expository Insight:

The phrase "your sleep will be sweet" (Hebrew: shenatekha na'imah, נְעִימָה שְׁנָתֶךָ, Strong's H8142 and H5273) signifies a state of peaceful rest. This rest comes not from external security but from an inner trust in God. Fear often stems from uncertainty or lack of control, but wisdom helps us entrust our concerns to God.

Application:

When we embrace wisdom, our minds are at peace, allowing us to rest without fear of the unknown. This peace is a powerful testimony to the value of godly wisdom in our lives, enabling us to live with calm assurance regardless of circumstances.

4. Protection from Sudden Terror

Wisdom not only protects us from internal anxiety but also provides confidence in the face of external dangers. Proverbs 3:25-26 reassures believers that they need not fear "sudden terror" or "the ruin of the wicked."

Verse Reference:

"Do not be afraid of sudden terror or of the ruin of the wicked, when it comes, for the Lord will be your confidence and will keep your foot from being caught." — Proverbs 3:25-26

Expository Insight:

The phrase "the Lord will be your confidence" (Hebrew: Yahweh mihnekha, מִחְנֶךָ יְהוָה, Strong's H3068 and H4009) underscores that our trust is ultimately placed in God, not in worldly circumstances. The assurance that God will "keep your foot from being caught" signifies divine protection, suggesting that wisdom aligns us with God's protective guidance.

Application:

In times of crisis or uncertainty, wisdom rooted in God provides inner stability, enabling us to respond without panic. Trusting in God allows us to face life's challenges courageously, knowing that He is in control and will sustain us.

5. Wisdom's Role in Providing Self-Control and Discernment

One of the benefits of wisdom is the development of self-control, which prevents impulsive actions that may lead to harm. Wisdom empowers us to make choices that reflect God's righteousness rather than reacting emotionally.

Verse Reference:

"A fool gives full vent to his spirit, but a wise man quietly holds it back." — Proverbs 29:11

Expository Insight:

The contrast between the "fool" and the "wise man" highlights wisdom's role in fostering self-restraint. While the fool acts on impulse, the wise person exercises discernment, reflecting a life grounded in God's guidance.

Application:

By embracing wisdom, we learn to act thoughtfully, considering the consequences of our actions. This self-control contributes to overall stability and well-being, preventing regrets and building a life of consistent integrity.

6. The Enduring Peace Found in Wisdom

The ultimate reward of a life rooted in wisdom is peace—a peace that the world cannot give, as it originates from a deep relationship with God. This peace is not dependent on external circumstances but is a result of abiding in God's truth.

Verse Reference:

"Great peace have those who love your law; nothing can make them stumble." — Psalm 119:165

Expository Insight:

The phrase "great peace" (Hebrew: shalom rav, שָׁלוֹם רָב, Strong's H7965 and H7227) implies complete or abundant peace. Those who love God's law, and therefore live by wisdom, experience a profound sense of security that remains unshaken by adversity.

Application:

Wisdom produces a peace that endures through life's ups and downs. This peace is a gift from God, providing a stable foundation that keeps us grounded even in turbulent times.

Embracing Wisdom as Our Security

Living a life grounded in godly wisdom offers personal security, emotional stability, and well-being that surpasses worldly solutions. Proverbs 3:21-26 assures us that those who pursue wisdom are not only guided in their daily choices but are also protected from the anxieties and fears that trouble others. When we keep wisdom and discretion close, we can walk through life securely, find rest in God's protection, and experience peace that is beyond human understanding.

Final Reflection:

In a world filled with uncertainties, godly wisdom provides believers with the assurance and peace needed to face life's challenges. By embracing wisdom, we align ourselves with God's truth, finding confidence and security in His promises.

CHAPTER 08

REJECTING FOLLY

"But whoever fails to find me harms himself; all who hate me love death."

— Proverbs 8:36

Introduction: The High Stakes of Wisdom and Folly

In the book of Proverbs, wisdom and folly are frequently contrasted, emphasizing the life-giving nature of wisdom and the destructive consequences of ignoring its counsel. Proverbs 8:36 starkly warns that rejecting wisdom is not a neutral choice; it's one that leads to "harm" and even "death." This chapter will explore the dangers of choosing folly over wisdom, drawing on biblical examples and principles to illustrate the consequences of such choices. We'll examine how rejecting wisdom's guidance brings not only personal suffering but often impacts communities and societies.

1. The Nature of Folly and Its Dangers

Proverbs often depicts folly as an aggressive force that leads individuals away from a fulfilling and righteous life. Folly is described as short-sighted, impulsive, and reckless, contrasting sharply with the careful, discerning nature of wisdom.

Verse Reference:

"The wise store up knowledge, but the mouth of a fool invites ruin." — Proverbs 10:14

Expository Insight:

The Hebrew term for "fool" (kesil, כְּסִיל, Strong's H3684) implies someone who lacks moral sense, not merely someone lacking intellect. In biblical terms, a fool is someone who disregards God's wisdom and pursues selfish desires, leading to ruin. "Invites ruin" reflects the Hebrew idea of "crushing" or "destruction" (mehitah, מְחִתָּה, Strong's H4288), emphasizing that folly attracts inevitable negative consequences.

Application:

Recognizing the nature of folly as more than just ignorance helps us understand why it is so dangerous. Folly not only disregards God's wisdom but actively opposes it, leading to decisions that harm oneself and others. To avoid folly, one must be attentive to wisdom's voice and diligent in following godly principles.

2. Rejecting Wisdom as a Path to Self-Destruction

When individuals reject wisdom, they become vulnerable to the harmful consequences of their choices. Proverbs 8:36 teaches that those who "fail to find" wisdom or "hate" it actively choose a path of self-inflicted harm.

Verse Reference:

"But whoever fails to find me harms himself; all who hate me love death." — Proverbs 8:36

Expository Insight:

The word for "harms" here (hamas, חָמַס, Strong's H2554) signifies violence or wrong-doing that rebounds on oneself. Rejecting wisdom is portrayed as an act that generates inner turmoil and eventual destruction. To "hate" wisdom means to reject its moral authority, and this hatred symbolizes a deeper resistance to God's guidance.

Application:

Ignoring wisdom has repercussions that extend beyond immediate choices, often leading to a cycle of poor decisions and suffering. The imagery of "loving death" symbolizes a life estranged from God, ultimately leading to spiritual separation. Choosing wisdom, therefore, is choosing life, both in a moral sense and in terms of the quality and peace of one's life.

3. Folly as a Source of Societal Breakdown

While folly impacts individuals, its effects often extend to communities and nations. When societies ignore wisdom, embracing injustice, selfishness, and moral decay, they inevitably suffer breakdowns in order, justice, and prosperity.

Verse Reference:

"Righteousness exalts a nation, but sin is a reproach to any people." — Proverbs 14:34

Expository Insight:

The word for "reproach" (hesed, חֶסֶד, Strong's H2617) often denotes disgrace or shame. When a society embraces sin over righteousness, it loses the stability and honor that come from wise and just governance. Folly, therefore, is not only a personal failing but a community-wide danger when unchecked.

Application:

History has shown that nations grounded in principles of justice, wisdom, and righteousness tend to experience greater stability. On the other hand, societies that abandon these principles often face internal conflict, corruption, and decline. As individuals, rejecting folly and choosing wisdom contribute positively to our communities and the world around us.

4. Biblical Examples of Rejecting Wisdom

The Bible presents several powerful narratives illustrating the consequences of rejecting wisdom. From Adam and Eve's choice in the Garden of Eden to King Saul's disobedience, these examples serve as warnings about the high cost of folly.

Example 1: Adam and Eve's Choice in Eden

Verse Reference:

"So the Lord God said, 'Behold, the man has become like one of Us, knowing good and evil; and now, lest he put out his hand and take also of the tree of life, and eat, and live forever'…" — Genesis 3:22

Expository Insight:

Adam and Eve's decision to eat from the Tree of Knowledge reflects the temptation of self-reliance over divine wisdom. By rejecting God's command, they not only brought suffering upon themselves but also introduced sin and death into the world. The Hebrew word for "knowledge" (da'ath, דַּעַת, Strong's H1847) signifies not merely information but an experiential understanding, something they sought without the guidance of God's wisdom.

Application:

Adam and Eve's story teaches that the desire for wisdom apart from God leads to devastating consequences. The lure of independence and self-determination remains a common temptation, yet wisdom calls us back to dependence on God's perfect will.

Example 2: King Saul's Rejection of God's Commands

Verse Reference:

"But Samuel replied: 'Does the Lord delight in burnt offerings and sacrifices as much as in obeying the Lord? To obey is better than sacrifice, and to heed is better than the fat of rams.'" — 1 Samuel 15:22

Expository Insight:

King Saul's repeated disobedience reflects a disregard for God's wisdom in favor of self-interest. The Hebrew word for "obey" (shama', שָׁמַע, Strong's H8085) means to listen with the intent to act. Saul's failure to obey led to the loss of his kingdom, emphasizing that wisdom in leadership requires humility and submission to God's commands.

Application:

Saul's life demonstrates the downfall of leaders who ignore wisdom in favor of personal gain. His story serves as a caution for anyone in a position of influence, reminding us that true success comes from adherence to godly principles, not ambition or ego.

5. The Hope and Promise of Embracing Wisdom

While rejecting wisdom has severe consequences, the Bible also offers hope for those who seek wisdom earnestly. The call to embrace wisdom is an open invitation, promising life, peace, and the favor of God.

Verse Reference:

"For those who find me find life and receive favor from the Lord." — Proverbs 8:35

Expository Insight:

The Hebrew word for "favor" (ratson, רָצוֹן, Strong's H7522) denotes divine goodwill and grace. Finding wisdom is associated with receiving God's blessing and experiencing a fulfilling life. This "favor" implies a closeness with God that provides both guidance and protection.

Application:

Turning away from folly and embracing wisdom is the path to spiritual renewal and fulfillment. While folly leads to a downward spiral, wisdom lifts us up, bringing life and joy. The promise of life to those who embrace wisdom emphasizes the profound impact wisdom has on our relationship with God.

The Urgency of Choosing Wisdom Over Folly

Rejecting folly is not simply about avoiding poor decisions; it's about choosing a life aligned with God's design and purposes. Proverbs 8:36 warns that rejecting wisdom is akin to embracing death, for folly leads to destruction both in this life and eternally. In embracing wisdom, we find a path of life, security, and joy. Wisdom calls us to choose not only the practical benefits of sound judgment but also the spiritual depth that comes from a relationship with God.

As we heed wisdom's call, we avoid the harm that comes from folly and walk securely in God's favor, bringing light to ourselves, our communities, and ultimately, to the world.

Understanding Proverbs 8:32-36 — The High Stakes of Loving Wisdom

"Now then, my children, listen to me; blessed are those who keep my ways. Listen to my instruction and be wise; do not disregard it. Blessed are those who listen to me, watching daily at my doors, waiting at my doorway. For those who find me find life and receive favor from the LORD. But whoever fails to find me harms himself; all who hate me love death."

— Proverbs 8:32-36

The Vital Choice Between Wisdom and Death

Proverbs 8 culminates with a powerful declaration about the consequences of rejecting wisdom. Here, Wisdom speaks in the first person, urging listeners to "listen," "keep my ways," and "find me," emphasizing that the choice to pursue wisdom is directly tied to one's spiritual, emotional, and physical well-being. This passage concludes with a striking warning: "all who hate me love death" (Proverbs 8:36). The stark juxtaposition of life and death here is not merely metaphorical but represents the profound spiritual reality that choosing wisdom leads to life, while rejecting it brings self-inflicted harm and death.

1. The Invitation to Listen and Be Blessed (Proverbs 8:32-34)

In verses 32-34, Wisdom extends an invitation to heed her instruction. The passage opens with a blessing for those who "keep my ways" (v. 32) and who "listen to my instruction and be wise" (v. 33). Here, Wisdom is not only offering guidance but framing it as a path to blessing and fulfillment.

Expository Insight:

The phrase "keep my ways" suggests more than mere acknowledgment; it means to cherish, adhere to, and walk in wisdom's principles. The Hebrew word used for "keep" (shamar, שָׁמַר, Strong's H8104) implies careful observance and protection. This term also appears in covenantal contexts, where "keeping" commands signifies faithfulness to God. Wisdom's instruction, therefore, is a path that aligns with covenantal faithfulness, reflecting a life committed to God's ways.

Application:

Choosing to "keep" wisdom's ways requires daily diligence, reflecting the disciplined pursuit of a life rooted in godly principles. Wisdom offers not only moral guidance but a promise of blessedness to those who seek her. This invitation is a call to prioritize wisdom as a foundational aspect of life, much like one would prioritize faithfulness to God.

2. The Reward of Finding Wisdom: Life and Favor (Proverbs 8:35)

Verse 35 emphasizes that those who find wisdom find "life" and "favor from the LORD." This reward suggests that wisdom is not just a philosophical ideal but a practical source of divine blessing, including well-being, peace, and joy.

Expository Insight:

The Hebrew word for "life" (chay, חַי, Strong's H2416) here encompasses more than physical existence; it refers to a fullness of life that includes spiritual vitality and purpose. Additionally, "favor" (ratson, רָצוֹן, Strong's H7522) implies a state of being pleasing to God and receiving His grace. Thus, the pursuit of wisdom is associated with a life that aligns with God's goodwill and divine grace.

Application:

Pursuing wisdom is a pursuit of abundant life, in which one not only survives but thrives under God's guidance. The concept of "finding life" implies that wisdom brings clarity, purpose, and alignment with God's design. This divine favor, or grace, becomes a stabilizing force, empowering believers to live fulfilled lives in harmony with God's will.

3. Rejecting Wisdom: The Harm of Folly (Proverbs 8:36)

Verse 36 warns of the destructive consequences of failing to find wisdom. The phrase "whoever fails to find me harms himself" suggests that rejecting wisdom is not a neutral act; it actively brings about self-destruction. Here, wisdom implies that rejecting her guidance leads directly to personal harm, both spiritually and physically.

Expository Insight:

The Hebrew term for "harm" (hamas, חָמָס, Strong's H2554) denotes violence or corruption. In this context, the term implies a self-inflicted injury, highlighting that those who disregard wisdom's counsel undermine their own well-being. This term can also denote moral decay, illustrating that rejecting wisdom corrupts one's inner character, leading to a life void of integrity and soundness.

Application:

Rejecting wisdom results in self-destructive patterns, where one's choices bring about personal turmoil and ruin. This harm isn't merely circumstantial but is a consequence of abandoning God's established order. Embracing wisdom aligns us with God's moral design, whereas rejecting it leads to instability, inner conflict, and ultimately, separation from life's true purpose.

4. "All Who Hate Me Love Death" — The Ultimate Consequence (Proverbs 8:36)

The final clause, "all who hate me love death," is perhaps the most striking statement in this passage. Here, death is presented not just as an inevitable outcome but as a chosen consequence for those who reject wisdom. This phrase implies that turning away from wisdom is an embrace of everything opposed to life and godliness.

Expository Insight:

The term "hate" (sane, שָׂנֵא, Strong's H8130) in Hebrew often implies an intense aversion or rejection. In the context of Proverbs, hatred for wisdom represents a conscious choice to disregard God's order. Meanwhile, "death" (mavet, מָוֶת, Strong's H4194) here symbolizes spiritual and moral ruin, not merely physical death. This choice to "love death" is a spiritual state marked by separation from God and from the life He offers.

Theological Meaning:

In rejecting wisdom, individuals essentially reject God's authority, opting instead for a life marked by spiritual darkness. Theologically, this choice signifies separation from God, aligning one's heart with the ways of destruction rather than the ways of life. Thus, the concept of "death" here refers to a state of spiritual alienation—a life devoid of the divine connection that brings wholeness, purpose, and peace.

Application:

The decision to embrace wisdom or folly is, ultimately, a decision to choose between spiritual life and death. Those who "hate" wisdom are essentially choosing a path that leads away from God's life-giving presence, opting instead for separation from Him and a life that lacks true meaning. This passage invites reflection on our attitudes toward wisdom, urging us to embrace it wholeheartedly and avoid the self-destructive allure of rejecting it.

Biblical Examples of Choosing Folly Over Wisdom

Example 1: The Israelites in the Wilderness

The Israelites repeatedly rejected God's wisdom by complaining and rebelling, despite witnessing His miraculous provisions.

Verse Reference:

"And the LORD said to Moses, 'How long will this people despise me? And how long will they not believe in me, in spite of all the signs that I have done among them?'" — Numbers 14:11

Their rebellion led to forty years of wandering in the wilderness, symbolizing a life marked by struggle, stagnation, and spiritual death. Their story serves as a powerful reminder of the consequences of rejecting God's guidance.

Example 2: King Saul's Disobedience

King Saul consistently disregarded God's instructions, preferring his own understanding over divine wisdom. His final rejection of God's counsel led to his demise.

Verse Reference:

"Because you have rejected the word of the LORD, he has also rejected you from being king." — 1 Samuel 15:23

Saul's fall from kingship symbolizes the ultimate consequence of hating wisdom—loss of purpose, power, and God's favor. His story exemplifies the dangers of loving "death" through a rejection of wisdom.

Choosing Life Through Wisdom

Proverbs 8:32-36 presents a stark contrast between life and death, emphasizing that these choices are defined by one's attitude toward wisdom. Embracing wisdom aligns us with God's order and blessing, while rejecting it brings ruin and spiritual separation. Through careful study and reflection, we see that wisdom is more than intellectual knowledge—it is a life-giving connection with God, who is the ultimate source of wisdom.

Key Takeaways:

1. Listening to Wisdom Brings Blessing: Those who seek wisdom actively find life and God's favor.

2. Rejecting Wisdom Leads to Harm and Death: Turning away from wisdom is a choice to embrace self-destructive patterns and spiritual separation.

3. A Call to Commitment: The passage invites us to make a commitment to daily pursue wisdom, aligning our lives with God's will and avoiding the lure of folly.

In the end, Proverbs 8 challenges us to take seriously the invitation to wisdom and the warning against rejecting it. The choice is set before us: to embrace life through wisdom or to fall into the snares of folly and experience the spiritual and moral consequences of "loving death."

Socrates, the Practice of Death, and the Wisdom of Proverbs

"But whoever fails to find me harms himself; all who hate me love death."

— Proverbs 8:36

The connection between wisdom and life is profound, with ancient thinkers across different cultures exploring the relationship between wisdom, life, and death. In the Hebrew Bible, the book of Proverbs frequently contrasts wisdom with folly, associating wisdom with life and folly with death. Similarly, in ancient Greek philosophy, Socrates and Plato's exploration of death is central to understanding their view of wisdom. Socrates, known for his teachings on the "practice of death," offers a philosophical perspective on life, death, and wisdom that shares an unexpected resonance with biblical themes.

This chapter will delve into the intersection between Socratic philosophy and the wisdom found in Proverbs. By examining both the Bible and Greek philosophy, we can uncover a shared pursuit of ultimate truth, life's meaning, and an understanding of how the wise approach life and death.

1. The Socratic "Practice of Death" and the Pursuit of Truth

In Plato's Phaedo, Socrates famously describes philosophy as a "practice of death." This concept does not imply a literal pursuit of death but rather signifies the philosopher's commitment to separating the soul from the body's desires and fears, seeking the ultimate truth that transcends the physical realm. Socrates viewed death as a release of the soul from the body, enabling it to attain pure knowledge and ultimate reality.

Philosophical Insight:

In his reasoning, Socrates taught that wisdom comes through the soul's purification from bodily distractions. The "practice of death" involves self-discipline, focus, and detachment from material concerns, enabling a person to seek truth in its highest form. Socrates argued that only by confronting and overcoming the fear of death could one gain wisdom. Thus, his "practice of death" represents a metaphorical death to the desires and illusions of this world in order to understand a higher reality.

Comparison to Proverbs:

The book of Proverbs also emphasizes a similar principle: wisdom is achieved when one seeks truth and understanding beyond earthly concerns. For example,

Proverbs 8 describes wisdom as a divine attribute that existed before the creation of the world, something pure and eternal. Just as Socrates believed that wisdom leads one to the highest truth, Proverbs portrays wisdom as a path that aligns individuals with God's ultimate truth and order.

"For those who find me find life and receive favor from the LORD. But whoever fails to find me harms himself; all who hate me love death." — Proverbs 8:35-36

In this passage, the Bible suggests that those who reject wisdom harm themselves and metaphorically "love death." Proverbs' version of "death" is not just a cessation of life but a condition of spiritual and moral separation from God. Just as Socrates viewed ignorance as a form of spiritual darkness, Proverbs warns of the perilous consequences of disregarding wisdom.

2. The Fear of Death: A Barrier to Wisdom in Proverbs and Plato's Philosophy

Both Proverbs and Greek philosophy address the role of fear—particularly the fear of death—in the pursuit of wisdom. In Phaedo, Socrates implies that the philosopher's soul must overcome the fear of death to attain pure knowledge. To fear death, he argued, is to cling to the physical life excessively and to remain entrapped by bodily concerns, which hinders one's spiritual enlightenment.

Philosophical Perspective:

In Greek philosophy, fear is often seen as an obstacle to wisdom. Plato teaches that it binds the soul to the physical world and prevents individuals from pursuing true knowledge. According to Socrates, to live in wisdom is to transcend the fear of death, to rise above the material distractions, and to engage fully with the life of the soul.

Theological Parallel in Proverbs:

In Proverbs, the "fear of the Lord" is foundational for wisdom. This concept signifies a profound respect and reverence for God rather than a paralyzing fear. Proverbs 9:10 states, "The fear of the LORD is the beginning of wisdom, and knowledge of the Holy One is understanding." Here, the biblical view is that fearing God, rather than fearing death or physical loss, leads to true wisdom. This "fear" reorients the person toward God's eternal reality, liberating them from fears rooted in worldly anxieties and aligning them with divine purpose.

Thus, both Socrates and the biblical tradition emphasize that true wisdom requires a transcendent perspective, freeing oneself from the fear of death or attachment to the material world. For Proverbs, the "fear of the Lord" is a reorientation away from earthly fears and desires, focusing one's heart and mind on God, the source of all wisdom.

3. Wisdom as a Guide for Righteous Living: Socrates and Proverbs on Moral Virtue

In both Socratic and biblical traditions, wisdom serves as a guide for righteous living, shaping moral and ethical conduct. Socrates saw wisdom as foundational to virtue, arguing that only the wise can truly live a virtuous life. In Plato's Republic, he suggests that wisdom enables a person to understand justice, courage, and temperance, aligning themselves with the Good.

Philosophical Insight on Wisdom and Virtue:

For Socrates, wisdom is intimately connected to moral character. In his view, the pursuit of wisdom naturally leads to ethical behavior because a truly wise person recognizes what is genuinely good and aligns their actions accordingly. Socrates' ethical philosophy suggests that wisdom is not simply knowledge but an application of understanding to live in harmony with the highest Good.

Wisdom and Righteousness in Proverbs:

Similarly, Proverbs teaches that wisdom leads to righteousness and upright living. Proverbs 8:20-21 personifies wisdom as saying, "I walk in the way of righteousness, along the paths of justice, bestowing a rich inheritance on those who love me and making their treasuries full." In Proverbs, wisdom provides moral clarity, guiding believers to act justly and righteously. This biblical wisdom transcends mere knowledge, encouraging believers to live in harmony with God's will and to exhibit integrity, justice, and compassion in their interactions with others.

Both Socrates and Proverbs affirm that wisdom is not just intellectual; it is inherently practical, transforming the way one lives. Wisdom brings moral insight, which enables individuals to align with higher principles—whether these principles are understood as the Good (in Platonic terms) or God's will (in biblical terms).

4. The Relationship Between Wisdom and Death: Life Beyond the Physical Realm

The culmination of both Socratic and biblical wisdom traditions is the recognition that true life exists beyond the physical realm. For Socrates, death represented a passage to a greater reality, where the soul would encounter ultimate truth. His philosophical "practice of death" thus reflects a belief that true wisdom is found by seeking this transcendent life rather than clinging to the temporary, material world.

Philosophical Perspective on Life and Death:

Socrates argued that the wise person embraces death not out of despair but out of a recognition that the soul's purpose transcends physical existence. In Phaedo, he states, "The one aim of those who practice philosophy in the proper manner is to practice for dying and death." For Socrates, wisdom reveals that the soul's true life begins only after it is freed from the constraints of the body.

Proverbs on Wisdom and Life Beyond Death:

In Proverbs, a similar concept exists, albeit with a distinctly theological foundation. The text teaches that wisdom leads to life, not merely in a physical sense but in an eternal and spiritual sense. Proverbs 8:35-36 declares, "For those who find me find life and receive favor from the LORD. But whoever fails to find me harms himself; all who hate me love death." Here, wisdom offers an invitation to participate in God's eternal reality, warning that those who reject wisdom choose a path that ultimately leads to spiritual death.

Proverbs emphasizes that those who pursue wisdom align themselves with life because wisdom reflects God's eternal truth. Thus, rejecting wisdom—like rejecting God—is akin to choosing a spiritual death, living a life devoid of purpose, direction, and ultimate meaning. This spiritual framework in Proverbs closely parallels Socratic thought, suggesting that a true understanding of life and death requires embracing wisdom's transformative power.

Embracing Wisdom, Embracing Life

Both Socratic philosophy and Proverbs offer profound insights into the relationship between wisdom, life, and death. For Socrates, wisdom means practicing detachment from worldly desires and preparing the soul for its ultimate journey. In Proverbs, wisdom is a divine path that leads to life and a deep relationship with God. Both traditions agree that wisdom transcends mere knowledge, transforming the way one lives and dies.

In choosing wisdom, both the philosopher and the believer embrace life—either by seeking truth that outlasts the physical world or by aligning oneself with God's eternal truth. Rejecting wisdom, by contrast, is a path that leads not only to moral and spiritual ruin but to a state of spiritual death. Thus, both the Hebrew Bible and Greek philosophy reveal that the stakes of wisdom go beyond this life, offering an invitation to true life that endures eternally.

CHAPTER 09

WISDOM AND CHRIST

"But to those whom God has called, both Jews and Greeks, Christ the power of God and the wisdom of God."

— 1 Corinthians 1:24

In Christian theology, the wisdom described in Proverbs 8 has been seen as a foreshadowing of Christ, who is both the "power of God" and the "wisdom of God." In this chapter, we will examine how the New Testament presents Jesus as the embodiment of divine wisdom and explore how Proverbs' description of wisdom finds its ultimate fulfillment in the person of Jesus Christ.

The relationship between wisdom and Christ has deep implications for understanding how God relates to the world and for recognizing the divine purposes that are revealed through Jesus. This chapter will connect passages from Proverbs with New Testament teachings, demonstrating how the pursuit of wisdom ultimately leads to a fuller revelation of Jesus as the perfect expression of God's wisdom.

1. Proverbs 8 and the Personification of Wisdom

In Proverbs 8, wisdom is depicted as a person, distinct yet intimately involved with God's creative work. Proverbs 8:22-30 illustrates wisdom as present with God from the beginning of creation, actively participating in the formation of the universe:

"The LORD brought me forth as the first of his works, before his deeds of old; I was formed long ages ago, at the very beginning, when the world came to be." — Proverbs 8:22-23

This passage is often interpreted as wisdom being both "with" God and playing an essential role in creation. Christian theologians have seen this personification of wisdom as a prefiguration of Christ, especially given the parallel in the Gospel of John, where Jesus is described as the "Word" through whom all things were made (John 1:1-3). Here, wisdom functions as the divine agent of creation, foreshadowing the role of Christ as God's expression in the world.

Strong's Concordance connects "wisdom" in Hebrew, ḥokmah (H2451), with practical and divine skill. In this context, Proverbs describes wisdom as a divine attribute, fundamentally part of God's nature, which aligns with the New Testament's revelation of Christ as the divine "Logos" (Greek: λόγος), or "Word."

2. Christ as the Embodiment of Divine Wisdom in the New Testament

The New Testament explicitly identifies Jesus with God's wisdom. In 1 Corinthians 1:24, Paul calls Christ "the power of God and the wisdom of God," asserting that the wisdom personified in the Old Testament is fully embodied in Jesus.

Wisdom and the Word of God

In John 1:1-3, Jesus is called the "Word" (Logos), who was with God in the beginning and through whom all things were made. The "Logos" serves as a bridge between God and creation, showing how Christ is both distinct from the Father and one with Him in divine purpose and essence. John's use of the term aligns with the portrayal of wisdom in Proverbs 8, which, like Christ, was present "in the beginning" and is closely associated with the act of creation.

"In the beginning was the Word, and the Word was with God, and the Word was God. He was with God in the beginning. Through him all things were made; without him nothing was made that has been made." — John 1:1-3

Through this parallel, the New Testament presents Christ as the eternal wisdom of God, incarnate in human form. As the Logos, Jesus personifies divine wisdom, living among humanity and revealing God's nature, will, and purpose. His life and teachings embody the wisdom that Proverbs portrays as integral to creation and to a life aligned with God.

Jesus' Role as Wisdom in Redemption

In 1 Corinthians 1:30, Paul explains that "Christ Jesus…has become for us wisdom from God—that is, our righteousness, holiness, and redemption." Here, Christ is not only wisdom in a metaphysical sense but also wisdom applied to the redemptive plan of God. Jesus brings God's wisdom to bear on humanity's salvation, becoming the means by which we are made righteous, holy, and redeemed.

In this sense, Jesus' sacrificial life and death reveal a deeper layer of divine wisdom—one that is paradoxical and even foolish by worldly standards but reveals God's profound and mysterious plan for reconciliation. Paul captures this in 1 Corinthians 1:25: "For the foolishness of God is wiser than human wisdom, and the weakness of God is stronger than human strength." God's wisdom, expressed in the humility and sacrifice of Jesus, transcends human understanding, inviting us into a relationship that goes beyond mere intellectual pursuit.

3. The Practical Impact of Christ as Wisdom

The wisdom of Christ is not just philosophical; it impacts how believers live and grow in righteousness. Jesus taught wisdom not as abstract knowledge but as a practical guide to living in harmony with God and others.

Teaching Through Parables and Proverbs

Jesus' parables often embody the wisdom found in Proverbs, teaching principles like humility, love, forgiveness, and generosity. These teachings mirror the lessons in

Proverbs, where wisdom guides behavior and reveals God's desires for humanity.

For example, in Matthew 7:24-27, Jesus tells the parable of the wise and foolish builders, emphasizing that wisdom leads to a stable foundation in life:

"Therefore everyone who hears these words of mine and puts them into practice is like a wise man who built his house on the rock… But everyone who hears these words of mine and does not put them into practice is like a foolish man who built his house on sand." — Matthew 7:24-27

Here, wisdom is about obedience to Jesus' words, reinforcing the idea that true wisdom is not just intellectual but practical, leading to actions grounded in God's truth. Like Proverbs, which stresses the practical benefits of wisdom, Jesus teaches that wisdom guides us toward a life built on a strong spiritual foundation.

Embodying the Wisdom of the Cross

The wisdom of Christ is most fully demonstrated in the "foolishness" of the cross. To the Greeks and Jews of Paul's time, the idea of a crucified Messiah was scandalous and incomprehensible. But in God's wisdom, this act of self-sacrifice was the pinnacle of divine love and wisdom, drawing humanity back to Himself. This "wisdom of the cross" calls believers to follow Christ's example of humility and service.

Philippians 2:5-8 describes Jesus' humility and obedience, encouraging believers to adopt a similar mindset:

"In your relationships with one another, have the same mindset as Christ Jesus: Who, being in very nature God, did not consider equality with God something to be used to his own advantage; rather, he made himself nothing by taking the very nature of a servant, being made in human likeness. And being found in appearance as a man, he humbled himself by becoming obedient to death—even death on a cross!" — Philippians 2:5-8

4. Pursuing Wisdom Through a Relationship with Christ

For believers, the pursuit of wisdom is inseparable from a relationship with Christ. To seek wisdom is ultimately to seek Christ Himself, who embodies God's perfect wisdom. As Colossians 2:3 states, "in whom are hidden all the treasures of wisdom and knowledge."

Through prayer, meditation on God's Word, and communion with Christ, believers are invited to deepen their understanding of divine wisdom. This pursuit aligns with

Proverbs' portrayal of wisdom as something to be earnestly sought after and cherished. In Christ, the promise of Proverbs 8:35-36 is fulfilled:

"For those who find me find life and receive favor from the LORD. But whoever fails to find me harms himself; all who hate me love death."

When we embrace Christ, we embrace the life-giving wisdom of God. Rejecting Christ is, in a sense, to reject wisdom and choose a path that leads away from God's life and favor. Thus, the call to seek wisdom in Proverbs becomes, for Christians, a call to seek Christ, who grants us the true wisdom that leads to eternal life.

Christ as the Ultimate Fulfillment of Wisdom

In both Proverbs and the New Testament, wisdom is portrayed as essential to understanding God and living in alignment with His purposes. The personification of wisdom in Proverbs finds its ultimate fulfillment in Jesus Christ, who embodies and reveals God's wisdom in human form. In Christ, we see wisdom's highest expression, a wisdom that not only guides but redeems, bringing us into a closer relationship with God.

As we seek wisdom, we are ultimately drawn closer to Christ, who invites us to share in the life and knowledge of God. Through Him, we find the fulfillment of all that Proverbs describes—security, understanding, and the favor of the Lord. In following Christ, we engage in the truest form of wisdom, embracing the divine life and truth that leads us to eternal communion with God.

Jesus as the Personification of Wisdom

"But to those whom God has called, both Jews and Greeks, Christ the power of God and the wisdom of God."

— 1 Corinthians 1:24

Throughout the Bible, wisdom is portrayed as a divine quality that belongs to God. In the New Testament, this divine wisdom is seen to be fully embodied in Jesus Christ, who is referred to as the "wisdom of God." Many early Christian thinkers, including St. Augustine, recognized that while the Father, Son, and Holy Spirit all share in divine wisdom, Scripture often uniquely identifies Jesus, the second person of the Trinity, with wisdom itself. This connection has profound implications for understanding Christ's nature, His role in creation, His redemptive work, and how believers can grow in divine wisdom through relationship with Him.

This chapter will explore how Jesus personifies wisdom, drawing on biblical passages, theological insights, and the teachings of the early church. Through understanding Jesus as the embodiment of God's wisdom, we gain a fuller picture of His divinity, His purpose, and His presence in both creation and redemption.

1. The Divine Origin of Wisdom and Its Personification in Jesus

Proverbs describes wisdom as a divine attribute, present with God in the act of creation:

"The Lord brought me forth as the first of his works, before his deeds of old; I was formed long ages ago, at the very beginning, when the world came to be." — Proverbs 8:22-23

Here, wisdom speaks as if it were a person, a characteristic uniquely integrated into God's nature. The personification of wisdom in Proverbs finds its New Testament counterpart in Christ. This connection is made explicit by Paul, who, in 1 Corinthians 1:24, calls Jesus the "wisdom of God." To the early church, this relationship indicated that Christ embodies wisdom in a way that is both distinct and fully divine.

St. Augustine elaborates on this concept, noting that while the Father, Son, and Holy Spirit all share in wisdom, it is the Son who is most frequently called "wisdom" in Scripture. In De Trinitate (On the Trinity), Augustine explains that this language points to the Son's unique role as the image of God and the agent of creation. Jesus, as divine wisdom, reveals God's character and purpose, mediating between God and humanity.

Strong's Concordance shows the Greek term sophia (G4678) used in the New Testament to signify "wisdom," encompassing both divine insight and the skillful ordering of the universe. In describing Christ as "sophia," the New Testament positions Him as the source and embodiment of God's ultimate wisdom, aligning closely with the portrayal of wisdom in Proverbs 8.

2. Christ's Role in Creation as Divine Wisdom

In John's Gospel, Jesus is referred to as the "Word" (Greek: Logos), who was with God from the beginning and through whom all things were made. John 1:1-3 presents Jesus as both distinct from and unified with God, embodying the wisdom that ordered the cosmos:

"In the beginning was the Word, and the Word was with God, and the Word was God. He was with God in the beginning. Through him all things were made; without him nothing was made that has been made." — John 1:1-3

This passage presents Jesus as the divine wisdom or "Logos" that was with God from the beginning. Just as Proverbs describes wisdom as instrumental in creation, John reveals that Jesus, as the Word, holds a central role in the act of creation. This aligns with the understanding of Jesus as the wisdom of God, actively involved in the formation of the universe.

Colossians 1:16-17 echoes this idea, stating that "all things have been created through him and for him. He is before all things, and in him all things hold together." The language used here reinforces the theological view that Christ, as wisdom, is not a mere participant in creation but the sustaining force behind it.

3. Wisdom in Redemption: Jesus as the Revealed Wisdom of God

Jesus not only embodies wisdom in creation but also in the divine plan of redemption. In 1 Corinthians 1:30, Paul asserts that "Christ Jesus… has become for us wisdom from

God—that is, our righteousness, holiness, and redemption." Through Jesus, God's wisdom is revealed in a way that transcends human understanding, particularly in His sacrificial death and resurrection. This act, which Paul describes as "foolishness to the Gentiles," is paradoxically the ultimate demonstration of God's wisdom (1 Corinthians 1:25).

By taking on human nature, Jesus bridged the gap between divine wisdom and human experience. His life, death, and resurrection embody a wisdom that surpasses worldly understanding. Philippians 2:5-8 describes Jesus' humility and obedience, reflecting the sacrificial love and redemptive power that characterize divine wisdom.

The Wisdom of the Cross

In the "wisdom of the cross," Jesus demonstrates a love that defies human logic, revealing God's wisdom in redemption. The cross, which seemed like weakness and defeat, was actually the power of God for salvation. This divine paradox is central to understanding the nature of wisdom as more than intellectual insight; it is the very expression of God's self-giving love.

Augustine commented on this aspect of divine wisdom, noting that Christ's humility and sacrifice reflect a wisdom that is counterintuitive to worldly values but consistent with God's character. Through Christ, wisdom is made accessible to humanity, offering redemption and a pathway to eternal life.

4. Living in Christ: Wisdom as a Guide for Christian Life

For believers, following Jesus as the wisdom of God means embracing His teachings and example. Jesus' life demonstrates that wisdom is not merely intellectual but deeply practical, impacting how we relate to God, others, and ourselves. As James 3:17 says, "The wisdom that comes from heaven is first of all pure; then peace-loving, considerate, submissive, full of mercy and good fruit, impartial and sincere."

Jesus' Teachings as Divine Wisdom

Jesus' teachings reveal the principles of godly wisdom: love, forgiveness, humility, and justice. His parables often encapsulate the wisdom described in Proverbs, providing insights on how to live righteously. For instance, the parable of the wise and foolish builders (Matthew 7:24-27) echoes Proverbs' emphasis on a solid foundation in wisdom.

"Therefore everyone who hears these words of mine and puts them into practice is like a wise man who built his house on the rock… But everyone who hears these words of mine and does not put them into practice is like a foolish man who built his house on sand." — Matthew 7:24-27

Here, Jesus illustrates that true wisdom involves applying God's word, aligning one's life with divine truth. His teachings reinforce the understanding that wisdom is both practical and transformative, leading to a life grounded in God's love and guidance.

The Indwelling of Christ as Wisdom

In Colossians 2:3, Paul describes Jesus as the one "in whom are hidden all the treasures of wisdom and knowledge." Believers are called to seek wisdom through their relationship with Christ, who, as the embodiment of divine wisdom, offers guidance, strength, and spiritual growth. Through prayer, meditation on Scripture, and communion with the Holy Spirit, believers deepen their understanding of God's wisdom.

5. The Theological Implications of Jesus as Divine Wisdom

Understanding Jesus as the personification of wisdom brings a deeper theological insight into the nature of God and the Trinity. Christ's embodiment of wisdom reveals God's desire to be known and understood by His creation. By identifying Jesus as the wisdom of God, Scripture presents a vision of God who is relational, loving, and actively engaged in guiding humanity toward Himself.

St. Augustine reflects on this mystery in De Trinitate, explaining that wisdom reveals the Son's unique role in the Trinity. While the Father, Son, and Holy Spirit are united in essence, it is the Son who is the "wisdom" made manifest. This theological understanding emphasizes Christ's role as the mediator of divine wisdom, drawing humanity into communion with God.

As the personification of divine wisdom, Jesus offers a pathway to understanding God's character, purpose, and redemptive plan. Through Jesus, wisdom is no longer abstract; it is incarnate, accessible, and transformative. To seek wisdom, therefore, is to seek Christ Himself, who embodies the fullness of God's knowledge, love, and power.

The call to wisdom found in Proverbs finds its ultimate fulfillment in the life, death, and resurrection of Jesus. By following Christ, believers enter into a relationship with the wisdom of God, growing in righteousness, understanding, and love. In Christ, wisdom is no longer merely a quality to be admired; it is a way of life, a guide to eternal truth, and the heart of God's revelation to humanity.

Where Did Jesus Get This Wisdom?

"Coming to his hometown he taught them in their synagogue, so that they were astonished, and said, 'Where did this man get this wisdom and these mighty works?'"

— Matthew 13:54

In Matthew 13:53–58, we encounter a fascinating interaction between Jesus and the people of Nazareth, His hometown. As Jesus preaches in the synagogue, He leaves His audience astonished at His wisdom and miraculous powers. Yet, their astonishment quickly turns to skepticism and offense. They cannot reconcile the wisdom and authority of Jesus with their familiarity with His background as the "carpenter's son." This episode in Jesus' life offers us insight into the source of His wisdom, the limitations of human understanding, and the unique nature of divine wisdom that is both profound and paradoxical.

This chapter will explore the theological implications of Jesus' wisdom, the prophetic insights of Isaiah that Jesus' hometown fulfills in their unbelief, and the New Testament's deeper revelation of Christ as the embodiment of both divine wisdom and power. Through examining these elements, we will gain a fuller understanding of how Jesus' wisdom, while divine, challenges and transcends human perceptions.

1. The Context of Unbelief: Jesus in His Hometown

In Matthew 13:53–58, Jesus returns to Nazareth, the town where He grew up, to preach in the synagogue. His teachings make a profound impact on His listeners, but rather than responding with faith, they react with doubt and scorn:

"Where did this man get this wisdom and these mighty works? Is not this the carpenter's son? Is not his mother called Mary? And are not his brothers James and Joseph and Simon and Judas? And are not all his sisters with us? Where then did this man get all these things?" — Matthew 13:54–56

The people of Nazareth recognize Jesus as possessing unusual wisdom and power, but they cannot accept that such qualities could be present in someone they know so well. Their familiarity with Jesus' family and humble origins blinds them to the reality of His divine identity. This response is a reflection of a common human tendency: to limit one's understanding of others based on external appearances and prior knowledge.

Fulfillment of Prophecy in Unbelief

Their reaction fulfills a prophecy Jesus had referenced earlier in Matthew, drawn from Isaiah: "you will indeed hear but never understand, and you will indeed see but never perceive" (Matthew 13:14; cf. Isaiah 6:9-10). Isaiah's prophecy highlights a condition of spiritual blindness and hardness of heart that hinders people from recognizing divine truth. In this instance, the people of Nazareth see and hear Jesus, but their understanding is blocked by preconceived notions. Their familiarity with Jesus' earthly background prevents them from perceiving His divine nature.

2. The Question of Jesus' Wisdom: Divine or Human?

The people of Nazareth ask, "Where did this man get this wisdom and these mighty works?" (Matthew 13:54). Their question underscores a profound tension: how can one who appears so ordinary demonstrate such extraordinary wisdom? This question—posed in a tone of disbelief—actually contains a deeper truth. Later, Paul would answer it by identifying Jesus as the "wisdom of God" (1 Corinthians

1:24). What the Nazarenes see as a mystery or anomaly is, in fact, the embodiment of divine wisdom.

Divine Wisdom Manifested in Humanity

Jesus' wisdom is not acquired through conventional means; it is intrinsic to His nature as the Son of God. The New Testament clarifies that Jesus' wisdom is not merely human wisdom but is a revelation of God's eternal wisdom made accessible in human form. The Greek word used for wisdom in the New Testament, sophia (Strong's G4678), implies both practical knowledge and divine insight. In the case of Jesus, this sophia transcends intellectual knowledge; it embodies God's eternal and redemptive plan, revealed uniquely in Christ.

Jesus as the Wisdom and Power of God

Paul's description of Jesus in 1 Corinthians 1:24 links both "wisdom" and "power" to Jesus' identity: "For those whom God has called, both Jews and Greeks, Christ the power of God and the wisdom of God." Here, Paul points to the counterintuitive nature of divine wisdom and power. Whereas human wisdom and power are often associated with intellect and dominance, divine wisdom is manifested in the humility and sacrifice of Jesus.

3. The Paradox of Divine Wisdom in Jesus' Ministry

Throughout His ministry, Jesus reveals a wisdom that is profoundly different from worldly wisdom. His teachings often contain paradoxes that challenge conventional thought, as in the Beatitudes (Matthew 5:3–12) and His teachings on loving enemies and serving others. These teachings demonstrate that divine wisdom involves humility, mercy, and self-sacrifice.

Wisdom Hidden from the "Wise"

In Matthew 11:25, Jesus offers a prayer of thanksgiving, saying, "I thank you, Father, Lord of heaven and earth, that you have hidden these things from the wise and understanding and revealed them to little children." Divine wisdom is not comprehended through human intellect alone but requires a humble heart open to revelation. The wise of this world, represented by the Pharisees and other religious leaders, often fail to grasp Jesus' wisdom because it does not conform to their expectations or their concepts of authority and righteousness.

The Power of Wisdom in Weakness

The wisdom of God revealed in Christ defies worldly expectations of power and success. Paul emphasizes this in 1

Corinthians 1:27: "But God chose the foolish things of the world to shame the wise; God chose the weak things of the world to shame the strong." Jesus' life and teachings embody a wisdom that subverts conventional power dynamics, offering an alternative vision of greatness rooted in servanthood and compassion.

4. The Ultimate Revelation of Wisdom in the Cross

The fullest expression of divine wisdom is seen in the cross of Christ. To the world, the crucifixion appears as defeat and foolishness, but to those with faith, it is the ultimate demonstration of God's wisdom and power. In the cross, God's wisdom is displayed through the paradox of life gained through death, strength revealed in weakness, and victory achieved through sacrifice.

"For the message of the cross is foolishness to those who are perishing, but to us who are being saved it is the power of God." — 1 Corinthians 1:18

The people of Nazareth could not comprehend the source of Jesus' wisdom because they expected wisdom to align with human power and honor. The cross subverts these expectations by revealing a wisdom that triumphs not through force but through love and self-giving.

The Hidden and Revealed Wisdom of God

Paul describes the cross as a "mystery that has been hidden" (1 Corinthians 2:7), a divine plan that only becomes clear through the eyes of faith. This hidden wisdom, which even the rulers of the age did not understand (1 Corinthians 2:8), is now revealed in Jesus. The cross, therefore, stands as the ultimate revelation of divine wisdom—a wisdom that challenges human understanding but brings redemption and life to those who believe.

5. Embracing Divine Wisdom: Lessons for Believers

As followers of Christ, we are called to seek and embody the wisdom that Jesus personifies. This wisdom involves not only intellectual insight but a heart transformed by God's love and truth. James 3:17 describes the nature of divine wisdom: "The wisdom that comes from heaven is first of all pure; then peace-loving, considerate, submissive, full of mercy and good fruit, impartial and sincere."

Learning to See Beyond Appearances

Like the people of Nazareth, we may be tempted to judge based on appearances or preconceived notions. However, true wisdom requires seeing with spiritual discernment, recognizing God's work even in unexpected places. Proverbs 3:5-6 reminds us, "Trust in the Lord with all your heart and lean not on your own understanding; in all your ways submit to him, and he will make your paths straight." This verse calls believers to rely on divine wisdom rather than their own understanding, aligning their lives with God's purposes.

Participating in the Life of Wisdom

By seeking Christ, the wisdom of God, believers can grow in godly wisdom. Colossians 2:2-3 encourages us to find wisdom and knowledge in our relationship with Christ: "My goal is that they may be encouraged in heart and united in love, so that they may have the full riches of complete understanding, in order that they may know the mystery of God, namely, Christ, in whom are hidden all the treasures of wisdom and knowledge."

In conclusion, the people of Nazareth asked the right question—"Where did this man get this wisdom?"—yet they failed to accept the answer. Jesus is the wisdom of God, a wisdom that challenges human expectations and offers a new way of understanding life, rooted in love, sacrifice, and the mystery of the cross. By embracing Christ as the wisdom of God, we are invited into a transformative relationship that reshapes our understanding and calls us to live out divine wisdom in our own lives. Through this wisdom, we find not only knowledge but a deeper relationship with God and a clearer path to the life He desires for us.

CONCLUSION

WALKING IN WISDOM

In Proverbs 8, wisdom speaks with urgency and warmth, calling out to humanity to pursue her, cherish her, and be transformed by her. This call is more than an invitation; it is a beckoning into a life aligned with God's purpose, a life that reflects His divine order. Through our study of wisdom, we have explored its foundations, its characteristics, its transformative power, and its embodiment in Christ. We have journeyed from the beginning of wisdom's call to its fulfillment in the person of Jesus, who is the "wisdom of God" (1 Corinthians 1:24). Now, as we conclude, we are called to put this knowledge into practice, to let wisdom shape our daily choices and bring us into closer communion with God and our fellow beings.

1. The Nature of Wisdom: Eternal and Divine

Proverbs 8 presents wisdom as more than a practical tool for successful living; it is woven into the very fabric of creation. Before the mountains were formed and the heavens stretched across the sky, wisdom was present, participating in God's creative work:

"The Lord possessed me at the beginning of His way, before His works of old. From everlasting I was established, from the beginning, from the earliest times of the earth." — Proverbs 8:22-23

Wisdom is foundational to the world God created, and when we walk in wisdom, we live in harmony with the divine order. By choosing wisdom, we are aligning ourselves with God's eternal purposes. This eternal aspect of wisdom reminds us that it is not merely human insight or common sense; it is God's perspective, timeless and unchanging. When we seek wisdom, we are seeking to understand the world as God understands it, to live with an awareness of His sovereign plan that spans beyond our limited perception.

2. Wisdom's Practical Benefits: A Guide for Daily Living

Throughout Proverbs, we see that wisdom provides guidance for every area of life. Proverbs 8 assures us that wisdom is practical and beneficial, leading to lives marked by stability, security, and fulfillment. We are told:

"Blessed are those who keep my ways...For whoever finds me finds life and obtains favor from the Lord." — Proverbs 8:32, 35

Wisdom enhances our relationships, guides our decisions, and strengthens our moral resolve. By following the path of wisdom, we avoid the pitfalls of impulsiveness, pride, and folly. Just as a skilled craftsman learns and hones his craft over time, a wise person learns to live with patience, discernment, and humility. Every moment offers us a choice between wisdom and folly, and each wise choice we make strengthens our character, builds our reputation, and draws us nearer to the abundant life that God intends for us.

The Wisdom of Humility

A crucial part of walking in wisdom is acknowledging our limitations and dependence on God. Proverbs 3:5-6 reminds us, "Trust in the Lord with all your heart and do not lean on your own understanding. In all your ways acknowledge Him, and He will make your paths straight."

Wisdom calls us to lean not on our own understanding but to trust in the Lord's guidance, allowing Him to direct our steps. This is a countercultural approach, as the world often glorifies self-sufficiency and independence. However, wisdom teaches us that true strength and security are found in humility and reliance on God's wisdom.

3. Rejecting Folly: A Call to Discernment

Throughout Proverbs, wisdom is contrasted with folly. Where wisdom brings life, folly leads to destruction. Proverbs 8:36 is direct: "But he who sins against me wrongs his own soul; all those who hate me love death." Here, we are warned of the high stakes in the pursuit of wisdom; to reject wisdom is to invite chaos, suffering, and death into our lives.

Folly represents a departure from God's design, a choice to live according to one's own understanding rather than God's. It is a rejection of the divine order, an insistence on our limited and often flawed perspective. The world often disguises folly as wisdom, celebrating material success, power, and pleasure as paths to fulfillment. However, Proverbs reveals that these pursuits, when divorced from God's wisdom, lead ultimately to emptiness and destruction. True discernment involves seeing beyond these illusions and recognizing the lasting value of a life guided by godly wisdom.

Learning to Discern in a Complex World

In today's world, we are bombarded with information and opinions, each claiming to offer insight or truth. Walking in wisdom requires us to be discerning, to test each idea against the standard of God's word. James 3:17 describes godly wisdom as "pure, then peaceable, gentle, open to reason, full of mercy and good fruits, impartial and sincere." This verse provides a litmus test for true wisdom. If a course of action or belief lacks these qualities, it may be rooted in folly rather than wisdom. By using God's word as our guide, we can learn to distinguish between truth and error, between godly wisdom and worldly deceit.

4. Christ as the Fulfillment of Wisdom

Proverbs 8 foreshadows the arrival of Jesus, the ultimate personification of wisdom. In the New Testament, Paul affirms that Jesus is "the wisdom of God" (1 Corinthians 1:24). Jesus embodies everything that wisdom represents: He is eternal, compassionate, righteous, and humble. Through His life and teachings, Jesus shows us the fullness of God's wisdom in action.

Wisdom's Ultimate Expression: The Cross

Nowhere is divine wisdom more powerfully displayed than in the cross. In 1 Corinthians 1:18, Paul writes, "For the message of the cross is foolishness to those who are perishing, but to us who are being saved it is the power of God." The cross defies human logic, yet it reveals the depth of God's love and the mystery of His redemptive plan. Through the cross, Jesus shows us that true wisdom is sacrificial, selfless, and redemptive. By embracing the cross, we align ourselves with a wisdom that seeks not self-interest but the good of others, a wisdom that ultimately brings us closer to God.

Following the Example of Christ

As followers of Christ, we are called to emulate His wisdom in our daily lives. This means making choices that reflect His love, humility, and righteousness. We are invited to participate in His work of redemption by living lives that embody the values of the kingdom. Wisdom is not just knowledge; it is a way of being—a life marked by the love, peace, and joy that come from a close relationship with God. By following Jesus, the personification of wisdom, we find ourselves transformed, becoming wise not by our own merit but through His grace.

5. A Lifelong Journey with Wisdom

The journey of wisdom is not a one-time decision; it is a lifelong pursuit. Each day, we face new choices, challenges, and opportunities to grow in wisdom. Proverbs 4:7 tells us, "The beginning of wisdom is this: Get wisdom. Though it cost all you have, get understanding." Wisdom is a treasure worth pursuing, a source of life and joy that continually renews and enriches us. The more we seek wisdom, the more we are drawn into the heart of God, who is the ultimate source of all understanding.

Walking Daily in Wisdom's Path

Walking in wisdom requires vigilance and intentionality. It is easy to be swayed by the pressures and distractions of daily life. However, as we draw closer to God through prayer, Scripture, and fellowship with other believers, we receive the strength and discernment needed to stay on the path of wisdom. Proverbs 8:34 assures us of the blessing that comes from daily communion with wisdom: "Blessed is the one who listens to me, watching daily at my gates, waiting beside my doors." This verse paints a picture of eager anticipation, a daily commitment to seek wisdom's counsel and to live by its guidance.

Embracing the Call of Wisdom

As we conclude our journey through Proverbs, we are reminded that the call of wisdom is more than an intellectual pursuit; it is a call to a transformed life. Wisdom invites us to walk in harmony with God, to live in alignment with His purposes, and to find joy, peace, and fulfillment in His presence. Wisdom is not a distant or unattainable ideal; it is accessible to all who seek it earnestly and faithfully.

Let us heed wisdom's call, rejecting the allure of folly and embracing the abundant life that God has prepared for us. As we walk in wisdom, we draw closer to God, to others, and to the purpose for which we were created. May our lives reflect the beauty of God's wisdom, shining as a light in a world that so desperately needs His truth. And may we, like Christ, embody the wisdom of God, bringing love, peace, and redemption to all those we encounter on our journey.

* 9 7 9 8 3 3 0 6 8 5 8 3 7 *